A Miscellany of
COOKS'
WISDOM

A Miscellany of

COOKS'
WISDOM
Diana Craig

RUNNING PRESS
Philadelphia, Pennsylvania

Canadian representatives: General Publishing Co., Ltd.,
30 Lesmill Road, Don Mills, Ontario M3B 2T6.
International representatives: Worldwide Media Services, Inc.,
115 East Twenty-Third Street, New York, New York 10010.

9 8 7 6 5 4 3 2 1
Digit on the right indicates the number of this printing.

Library of Congress Catalog Number 91-50612

ISBN 1-56138-092-X

A Miscellany of Cooks' Wisdom
Compiled by Diana Craig
Designed by Simon Jennings
Edited by Peter Leek
Picture research by Ben Jennings
Illustrations & engravings enhanced by Robin Harris

Produced, edited, and designed by Inklink,
Greenwich, London, England
Published in the United States by Running Press,
Philadelphia, Pennsylvania
Typeset in Garamond by Inklink
Printed in Hong Kong by South Seas International Press.

This book may be ordered by mail from the publisher.
Please add $2.50 for postage and handling.
But try your bookstore first!
Running Press Book Publishers
125 South Twenty-Second Street
Philadelphia, Pennsylvania 19103

A MISCELLANY OF

COOKS' WISDOM

TABLE OF

CONTENTS

ARRANGED IN FIVE CHAPTERS

*"Cookery is become an art,
a noble science . . ."*

From THE ANATOMY OF MELANCHOLY by
ROBERT BURTON, 1621

LIKE MOST WORKING WOMEN THAT HAVE A FAMILY to feed, I rarely have time to go from store to store, carefully selecting the best produce and then taking it home to cook with equal care and attention. Instead, I largely depend on what the local supermarket can supply in the way of quick foods or prepared meals, often snatched on my way home at the end of a busy day.

On browsing through old cookbooks, however, I glimpsed a world very different from my own. In the days when women generally did not work outside the home, they were able to devote much more of their time to domestic tasks. As guardians of their family's health and well-being, they took great pride in their skills as homemakers – and, as the kitchen is the heart of the home, it was vital to have a thorough knowledge of the art of honest home cooking.

In the pages of these books, I discovered a tradition of simple culinary wisdom – a wealth of tips, hints, and secrets that mothers passed on to their daughters so they could perform properly their wifely duties. This tradition represents an era of calm, ordered lives, of tasks done unhurriedly, without great expense or fuss, and without special equipment or expertise. Meals were served at the appointed times, marking one's steady progress through the day, and the cook's skill and economy meant that few ingredients, however lowly, went to waste.

Although we cannot return to those simpler days, there is much to be learned from the cooks of the past. Producing good food does not have to depend on luxury ingredients or having the latest gadgets. Above all, COOKING IS AN ACTIVITY TO BE SAVORED. If we only slow down a little, our time in the kitchen can be the most pleasant time of the day.

DIANA CRAIG

DEDICATED TO
GOOD NUTRITION
AND A WHOLESOME DIET.
LET WISDOM PREVAIL.

ONLY THE BEST

N OT EVEN THE MOST RESOURCEFUL COOK
can produce wonderful food if the basic
ingredients are inferior. An important part of the
cook's task is to choose the best and
freshest ingredients – and that means knowing
what to look for.

*"Tell me what you eat, and I shall tell you
what you are."*
JEAN ANTHELME BRILLAT-SAVARIN (1755-1826)

Robin the Bobbin, the big-bellied Ben,
He ate more meat than fourscore men;
He ate a cow, he ate a calf,
He ate a butcher and a half,
He ate a church, he ate a steeple,
He ate the priest and all the people!
A cow and a calf,
An ox and a half,
A church and a steeple,
And all the good people,
And yet he complained that his stomach wasn't full.

TRADITIONAL RHYME

HOW TO TELL GOOD BEEF

"The lean part of beef should be firm and elastic to the touch, free from moisture and unpleasant odour, and when recently killed, bright red in colour, but the colour gradually deepens until parts exposed to the air become almost mahogany coloured. The fat should be fairly firm and cream coloured.... A certain amount of fat is an indication of good quality.

Veal must be fresh killed to be good. The lean should be white, smooth and juicy; the fat, white, firm, and abundant. Stale veal is moist and clammy, the joints are flabby, and there is a faint musty smell."

From MRS BEETON'S COOKERY BOOK, 1914

MUTTON & LAMB

Mutton should be bright red in color, and of a fine grain, with firm, white fat.

Lamb should be of a paler color, with white fat, and should feel smooth and firm to the touch. A yellowish tinge to the fat shows excessive age.

PORK, HAM, & BACON

At one time, in some countries, fresh pork was only sold during the cooler months of the year, due to the widespread belief that it was best avoided throughout the summer (from May to August), when the weather was most likely to be warm.

The best pork has close-grained meat, without too much fat. The fat should be pinkish-white in color, and firm to the touch. The skin should be thin, pliable, smooth, and free of hairs (in older pigs, the skin tends to thicken and coarsen).

When selecting ham and bacon, choose pieces in which the lean is bright red and firm, and the fat white. The fat on bacon should not have a green or yellow tinge.

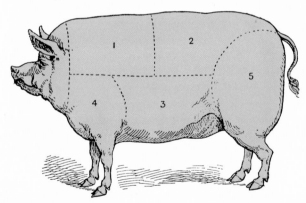

"To test the sweetness of a ham, run a sharp knife or skewer into it close to the bone, and if when withdrawn it has an agreeable odour, the ham is good; if the blade has a greasy appearance and an offensive smell, the ham is bad."

From MRS BEETON'S COOKERY BOOK, 1914

THICKER THAN WATER

In the Upper Nile region, in Africa, the Nuer people thicken blood by boiling it or allowing it to coagulate, after which it can be roasted.

In Ireland, in the counties of Derry and Tyrone, layers of blood were left to coagulate and were preserved by being sprinkled with salt. The solidified blood could then be cut up into squares and eaten at times when other food was scarce. In Ireland, too, a kind of blood "pudding" known as "drisheen" is a traditional dish. A form of drisheen was being made back in the seventeenth century. According to a French traveller to the country, the peasants bled their cows and then boiled the blood with milk and butter from the same animal, seasoning the mixture with herbs, to make "one of their most delicious dishes."

Blood is the key ingredient, too, in the French *boudin*, a kind of sausage, and in the English equivalent, black pudding.

"To make Excellent Black-puddings. Take a quart of Sheeps-blood or Pigs-blood warm, and a quart of Cream: ten Eggs, the yolks and whites beaten well together. Stir all this liquor very well, then thicken it with grated Bread and Oat-meal finely beaten, of each a like quantity; with Beef suet finely shred and Marrow in little lumps. Season it with a little Nutmeg and Cloves and Mace mingled with Salt, Sweet Marjoram, Thyme and Pennyroyal shred very well together: some put in a few Currants. Mingle all this well, and pour it into a skin of cleansed Guts, tied at one end: then tie the other end, and boil the Puddings carefully."

From THE CLOSET OF SIR KENELM DIGBY OPENED, 1669

PENNYROYAL *(Mentha pulegium)*
Aromatic herb with hairy leaves
and small blue flowers.

HORSE TRADING

In nineteenth-century France, in order to improve the diet of the poor, attempts were made to encourage people to eat horsemeat. In 1855, the director of a veterinary college, one Monsieur Renault, held a tasting for a group of gourmets to compare the merits of horsemeat versus beef. The animal chosen for this experiment was a 23-year-old horse which had suffered from incurable paralysis; it was killed and the meat cooked in a similar way to beef. The tasters were impressed. Horse *bouillon* (stock), they pronounced, was superior to that of beef, and roast horse fillet better than roast beef fillet.

In 1868, in London, a similar dinner was given featuring such imaginatively named dishes as Roast Fillet of Pegasus, Patties of Bucephalus-marrow, and Lobster with Rosinante-oil Mayonnaise. Despite the cooks' creative efforts, however, the idea failed to catch on in England.

PEGASUS The winged horse of the Greek and Roman gods.

BUCEPHALUS The war-horse of Alexander the Great.

ROSINANTE Don Quixote's horse.

THE WALKING TEST

There was a simple way to tell whether your pig was fat enough to slaughter:

"If he can walk two hundred yards at a time, he is not well fatted. Lean bacon is the most wasteful thing that any family can use . . . The man that cannot live on solid fat bacon . . . wants the sweet sauce of labour, or is fit for the hospital."

From COTTAGE ECONOMY by WILLIAM COBBETT, 1822

I WONDER WHICH IS FATHER.

"Christmas is coming, the geese are getting fat . . ."
From A TRADITIONAL RHYME

HOW TO CHOOSE POULTRY & GAME

TURKEY

Check that the legs are smooth and black, the spurs (the horny projection just above the claws) short, the breast full, and the neck long. The eyes should be round and bright, the feet soft and supple. If the eyes are sunken and the feet are dry, the bird is stale.

CHICKEN

A young chicken should have smooth legs, with short spurs. When the bird is fresh, the vent (rear opening) is close and dark. White-legged chickens are generally preferred, for no reason except that the flesh is whiter.

GOOSE

A young goose has a yellowish bill and supple feet with few hairs on either. If the bill and feet have a red tinge, and are hairy, the bird is old; if the feet are dry, it is stale.

DUCKS

Both wild and tame ducks should have pliable feet, with a full, firm breast and clear skin.

PIGEONS

The bird's feet should be supple, and the vent close and hard.

GAME BIRDS

When choosing game birds, pull out a few feathers from the under part of the leg; if the skin is not discolored, the bird is fresh. Another test is to place your thumb into the beak, and hold the bird up by the jaw section: if this breaks, the bird is young, but if not, the bird is old and will need to be hung for longer to make it edible.

HARE AND RABBIT

A freshly killed hare is stiff and red; the cleft in the lip of a young hare is narrow, and the claws crack easily if turned sideways. If the hare is stale, its body will be supple and the flesh black in many parts. If the ears are tough and dry, the hare is old.

Rabbits may be judged in the same way. The claws in both animals should be smooth and sharp.

HOW TO CHOOSE FISH

Avoid any fish that looks watery or fibrous, or fish whose flesh has a blue or green tinge, as it is almost certainly stale.

"In every kind of fish the flesh should be thick and firm, the gills red and the eyes bright. If, on pressing the fingers on the flesh, the impression remains, the fish is stale. Freshness is best indicated by the smell. Medium-sized fish are generally preferable to those which are very large or very small."

From MRS BEETON'S COOKERY BOOK, 1914

OYSTERS

Oysters have not always been luxury items, as they are in most parts of the world today. They were once food for the poor, and in traditional English cooking were combined with meat in such dishes as Lancashire Hotpot – a hearty mutton, potato, and onion stew from the North of England. They also featured in Steak and Kidney Pudding, a steamed savory pudding consisting of a suet-pastry case filled with the meat and oyster mixture. This is one of the greatest of all English dishes, and was a speciality of London public houses, in particular the famous "Cheshire Cheese" in London's Fleet Street. Nowadays we usually prefer to eat oysters on their own, uncooked, with a squeeze of lemon and thin slices of brown bread and butter.

Traditionally, English oysters should only be eaten when there is an "r" in the month (from September to April) – but perhaps nineteenth-century oyster-eaters were not able to wait that long:

SUET The fat from around
beef or lamb kidneys.

Greengrocers rise at dawn of sun
August the fifth – come haste away
To Billingsgate the thousands run
'Tis Oyster Day! 'Tis Oyster Day!

From the EVERY-DAY BOOK by HONE, 1829

BILLINGSGATE The famous
London fish market.

CHOOSING VEGETABLES

When selecting vegetables, the rule is "freshest is best." If you cannot grow your own and have to buy your vegetables, choose ones that are crisp and firm, but not hard; avoid small vegetables, as these may be immature and so lacking in flavor. Also avoid the larger ones, as they are likely to be coarse in texture.

BRUSSELS SPROUTS
Choose sprouts that are firm and compact, and are a fresh green color. Avoid puffy sprouts, and any with a smudgy, dirty appearance, as that may well be a sign of plant lice.

CABBAGES
The heads should be solid with all but three or four wrapper leaves removed, and the stem cut close to the head. If the base of some of the outer leaves has separated from the stem, the cabbage may be strong-flavored and coarse.

CARROTS
Carrots should have a good color, and be firm and smooth. An excessive amount of leaf stems may mean that the carrots have large cores.

CAULIFLOWERS
Choose cauliflowers with white, clean, firm, and com-pact heads. Avoid any with spreading flower clusters or spotted and bruised curd.

CELERY
Good celery should be crisp enough to snap easily. Press lightly to test, and avoid celery with pithy, stringy stalks. Open the head to check for rot, insect damage, and the formation of seed stems.

CUCUMBERS
These should be firm, well-shaped, and deep green in color. Shriveled, withered cucumbers will be rubbery and bitter; puffy, yellow ones are old, and will have rubbery flesh and hard seeds, but they can used for some pickles.

LETTUCE
Lettuce should be crisp, without dead or discolored leaves that may be a sign of decay. Check for knob-like seed stems, as the lettuce may then taste bitter. Do not be too concerned about wilted outside leaves, as the interior should still be good.

MUSHROOMS
To test the quality of mushrooms: when stewing, put a silver coin into the pan and, if it turns black, discard the mushrooms for they are not fit to be eaten.

PEAS
Pods should be bright green and slightly velvety to the touch. Flat, dark green pods mean immature peas, and swollen pods, poorly colored, and flecked with grey, are a sign of age – the peas will be tough and lacking in flavor.

POTATOES
Potatoes should be smooth, shallow-eyed, and reason-ably clean. Avoid any that have a discolored, wilted, or leathery appearance, or have green patches. The green color develops when potatoes are exposed to light, and indicates the presence of a particular poison. Also avoid frozen potatoes: these may be wet, have dark rings below the surface and turn black when cooked.

SWEET POTATOES
Misshapen, cracked potatoes are not a good buy only because of wastage. Large, dark blotches on the outside, made up of smaller spots, are only skin-deep and do not affect the quality; real decay will be shown by soft, wet patches or dry, shriveled, sunken and discolored areas.

SQUASH
Summer squash should feel heavy for its size, be free of blemishes and have a rind that is easily punctured. Winter squash should also be heavy and free from blemishes, but the rind should be hard.

TOMATOES
These should be mature, firm, plump, and smooth, with a good color and no blemishes. Any tomatoes that are cracked must be used at once.

ZUCCHINI
Choose small, crisp zucchini. Avoid wilted ones, as these will have a poor flavor.

CHOOSING FRUIT

As a general guide, apples, pears, peaches, and other fruit that grows on trees, should be firm and free from blemishes or bruises. The fruit should be bought in small quantities, as it does not keep long at room temperatures. Pears, plums and apricots are best picked or bought when slightly under-ripe, and allowed to ripen indoors.

Good-quality citrus fruits will have bright, taut, and moist-looking skins; avoid any that look dry, or have blemishes or slight hollows in the skin.

When buying soft fruit, avoid any that are moldy; or, as soon as possible, separate the moldy ones from the others and discard.

"If you would have fruits to keep long, then let them not be over-ripe on the tree: and gather them about the first or last quarter of the moon."
From LAKE'S ALMANACK, 1628

APPLES
Choose fruit that is firm and has a good color. Immature apples will shrivel in storage, and over-ripe fruits are mealy and lacking in flavor. If there is slight scald – brown, irregular patches – on the skin, this will not affect the quality much. Scald is caused by gases given off during storage.

APRICOTS
Choose plump, firm, evenly colored fruit. Immature apricots are greenish-yellow, hard, slightly shriveled, and with a poor flavor. Ripe ones perish very quickly.

BANANAS

Those with the best flavor are harvested green. Good-quality fruits will have a good color, flecked with brown. Avoid any that are soft or have black patches. If the bananas have been allowed to become too cold, they will not ripen properly.

BLUEBERRIES AND HUCKLEBERRIES

These should be dry and clean, with a good, full color. Over-ripe fruit will look dull and lifeless, berries that have been kept too long will be dull and shriveled.

LEMONS

Choose heavy fruit with smooth skins. Avoid fruits that feel soft or spongy, or have decay at the stem end.

ORANGES

These should feel firm and heavy. Blemishes on the surface will not affect the quality, but avoid any fruits that are light and puffy or have badly creased skins.

PEACHES

If the fruit has a greenish ground color, it was picked too soon and will not ripen fully. Only choose very ripe peaches if they are going to be eaten immediately. Brown, circular spots on the skin mean decay, and this spreads rapidly.

PEARS

These should be firm but not hard. If they are soft at the base of the stem, they should be eaten at once. If they are wilted or shriveled, they have been picked too early to ripen and develop a full flavor.

Green fruits make sickness to abound
Use good advice to keep these sound
Give not thy lusts what they do crave
Lest thou unawares step into grave

From RANGER'S ALMANACK, 1627

PLUMS

Ripe plums are plump and will yield to slight pressure. Immature fruit is hard, shriveled, with a poor flavor and color. Over-ripe fruit is soft and leaks juice. A brownish color on the skin may be a sign of sunburn, and the flavor will probably be poor.

"All Plums are under Venus, and are like women, some better and some worse. As there is a great diversity of kinds, so there is in the operation of Plums, for some that are sweet moisten the stomach, and make the belly soluble: those that are sour quench thirst more, and bind the belly. The moist and waterish do sooner corrupt in the stomach, but the firm do nourish more, and offend less."

From the herbal by NICHOLAS CULPEPER, 1653

FRESH FROM THE TREE

Tradition has it that rain on St Swithin's Day (July 15th) "blesses and christens" apples, so they ripen. It was therefore best not to pick or eat them before then.

Apples are ready for picking when they will part easily from the tree. Pick them one by one, placing each gently in a lined basket.

The moon in the wane, gather fruit for to last,
But winter fruit gather when Michael is past,
Though scrumpers that love not to buy or to crave
Make some gather sooner – or else few to have.

From TUSSER'S FIVE HUNDRED POINTS OF GOOD HUSBANDRY, 1573

MICHAEL Michaelmas (the Feast of St Michael) on September 29th.

SCRUMP To gather windfalls, or to raid orchards.

TESTING THE FRESHNESS OF EGGS

THE WATER TEST
Lower an egg into a bowl of water. If it lies on its side, it is quite fresh, but if it stands on its end, it is less fresh. If it floats to the top, it is stale and you should throw it away.

THE AGE TEST
Put an egg into a glass of water. A fresh egg will sink all the way to the bottom. A three-week-old egg will lie nearly on its side, with its broader end up. A three-month-old egg will stand straight up, its wide end just showing. An egg that is even older will rise up, partly above the water.

THE TONGUE TEST
Place your tongue on the large end of the egg: if it feels warm, it is fresh.

THE CANDLE TEST
Hold an egg before a lighted candle or up to the light: if it looks clear, it is reasonably good; if opaque, it is stale; and if there is a black spot on the shell, it is useless and must be discarded.

SPOILING THE DISH
Never use an egg that is even slightly tainted, for it will spoil whatever dish it has been used in.

"Who can help loving the land [France] that has taught us six hundred and eighty-five ways to dress eggs?"
THOMAS MOORE (1779-1852)

THE BEST MILK

"Cow's milk is not good for them which have gurgulations in the belly, but it is very good for melancholy men, and for old men and children."
From the DIETARY OF HEALTH by ANDREW BOORDE, 1547

In warm weather, cows produce richer milk than in cold or wet weather, and milk provided in the morning is always richer than that of the evening. The last milk drawn at each milking, whatever the season or weather, is always richer than the first, and should be set aside for cream-making. When carrying milk from the cow to the dairy, it should be shaken as little as possible and poured very carefully into the pans.

"Things are seldom what they seem
Skim milk masquerades as cream."
W. S. GILBERT, 1836-1911

BUTTER TIME

Butter made in spring is said to be better than butter made in winter, May being the best month of all.

If you want to be successful in your butter-making, repeat the following charm three times:

> *Come butter come*
> *Come butter come*
> *Peter stands at the gate*
> *Waiting for a buttered cake*
> *Come butter come.*

From A CANDLE IN THE DARK, 1655

TESTING UNSALTED BUTTER

Butter can become rancid more quickly than other fats and oils; if it tastes at all rancid, it should not be used. Never be tempted to use even slightly sour butter, for it will taint the whole dish.

Butter may be unsalted (sometimes called "fresh" or "sweet") or salted to help it keep.

"[Butter] should smell deliciously, and be of an equal colour throughout. If it smells sour, it has not been sufficiently washed from the buttermilk. If it is veiny and open, it has probably been worked with a staler or inferior sort."

From MRS BEETON'S COOKERY BOOK, 1914

CHEESE

A mature cheese does not improve with keeping, so buy only sufficient for one or two days at a time. When choosing hard cheeses, avoid any that have cracks running from the edge to the middle, or in which there is a noticeable difference in color between the outer edge and the centre. These are signs that the cheese has begun to dry out.

Soft cheeses have even lower keeping properties than harder varieties, so buy in small quantities. When ripe, a soft cheese will be soft all the way through; if it is still a little under-ripe, allow it to mature for a day or two before serving.

Keep all cheeses at room temperature for at least one hour before serving, to allow their flavor to develop.

"Cheese that is good ought not to be too hard nor too soft, but betwixt both: it must be of good savour, not full of eyes, nor mites, nor maggots. Yet in High Germany the cheese which is full of maggots is called there the best cheese, and they will eat the maggots as fast as Englishmen do comfits."

From DIETARY OF HEALTH by ANDREW BOORDE, 1547

TESTING SALTED BUTTER

To test whether salted butter is still fresh, plunge a clean knife into the center of the mound; draw the knife out and, if it smells rancid or unpleasant, the butter is bad.

Betty Botter bought some butter,
But, she said, the butter's bitter:
If I put it in my batter
It will make my batter bitter,
But a bit of better butter
Will make my batter better.
So she bought a bit of butter
Better than her bitter butter,
And she put it in her batter
And the batter was not bitter.
So t'was better Betty Botter bought a bit
of better butter.

TRADITIONAL TONGUE TWISTER

FOR YOUR HEALTH

We now believe that bread made from stone-ground whole-wheat flour is the best for our health, but views in the ancient world were different. Siphilus, a writer on hygiene, was very clear about what was superior and what was inferior bread. First of all, he regarded bread made from wheat flour as better than barley bread. Refined (thoroughly sieved) wheat flour produced the most superior loaves, followed by ordinary flour, while unbolted (unsifted) flour made the poorest quality bread.

STOLEN DOUGH

In 1327, a London baker named John Brid devised a sly way to deceive the public. His customers used to bring their uncooked dough to him to be baked, and Brid would place it on a table next to him. The table contained a small trapdoor and, while Brid engaged the customer in conversation, an employee hidden under the table would furtively open the door and remove a piece of dough.

The remaining dough would be baked and returned to the customer, slightly but not noticeably lighter than before. The stolen pieces were then used in loaves that were sold back to the customers. When Brid was finally indicted, he was told that he had acted "falsely, wickedly, and maliciously; to the great loss of all his neighbors and persons living near."

CHAPTER TWO

ON THE SHELF

WHEN THE MARKETING HAS BEEN DONE, the next job for the cook is to store the various ingredients so that they will stay in peak condition until needed. Before the days of refrigerators and freezers, clever cooks knew all sorts of tricks to make even the most perishable foods stay fresher longer.

"Wilful waste makes woeful want."
TRADITIONAL SAYING

CANNED FOODS

The technique of preserving food by heating it in sealed cans was developed around the beginning of the nineteenth century. The first step was when Nicholas Appert, in France, discovered that various foods – meat, fruit, vegetables, and milk – would remain edible longer if heated and sealed in glass bottles. The jump from using glass bottles to cans was made by an Englishman, Bryan Donkin, who was involved in the ironworking industry. By 1812, Donkin had set up his own canning factory, and six years later it was producing cans of corned and boiled beef, meat and vegetable stews, carrots and soups.

In the United States, there were canning factories as early as 1817, but it was only after the Civil War that the canning industry was really able to flourish. During the war, the soldiers of the Union army were supplied with home-produced canned meat, oysters, and vegetables – but seemed to prefer imported French sardines, salmon and green peas!

"When fuel and food have been procured, the next consideration is, how the latter may be best preserved .... Much waste is often occasioned by the want of judgment or of necessary care in this particular."
From MRS BEETON'S COOKERY BOOK, 1914

DRIED FOODS

Drying has always been one of the main methods of preserving food, and in countries where the weather is either consistently hot, or cold and crisp, it has been particularly successful. In the Near East, an ancient way of drying dates, figs, and grapes was to bury them in the desert sand. Meat was beaten with stones to flatten it, and then left to dry in the sun.

In Scandinavian countries, fresh winds and cold air did the same job as the Mediterranean sun. Norwegian dried fish, known as *stokkfisk,* consisted of cod, gutted and hung up by the thousand to dry on wooden racks. Although it was cheap, and had impressive keeping qualities, any cook faced with preparing it had to have plenty of energy. According to a fourteenth-century merchant, *stokkfisk* ten to twelve years old needed to be beaten with a wooden hammer for one hour and soaked in warm water for a further two. The fish then had to be cooked and scoured, after which it could, at last, be eaten, either with mustard or coated in butter.

SALTED FOODS

Salting became especially important with the rise of Christianity. The eating of meat was forbidden during Lent, so Christians had to eat fish – and salted fish was often the only sort obtainable inland. In medieval times salt was expensive. The thrifty housewife therefore had to exercise care in choosing which animals to salt herself. The amount of salt needed could add as much as 40 per cent to the total cost, so it would only be worth curing a good, plump carcass. A tough, stringy animal would literally not be "worth its salt."

There were two ways of salting – brine-curing and dry-salting. Brine-cured meat was soaked in a strong solution of salt and water; dry-cured meat was buried in a bed of salt. Dry-salting produced good results; but it was very hard work pounding the lumpy medieval salt, and in noble households there was a servant called the "powderer" whose task it was to grind the salt with a huge mortar and pestle.

FROZEN FOODS

People have always known that keeping food really cold helped to preserve it. The problem was that they did not know how to make ice themselves and had to rely on nature's supply. The ancient Chinese stored naturally formed winter ice in icehouses, kept cool by evaporation; the emperors of sixteenth-century India sent out horsemen to bring back snow and ice to Delhi for their fruit-flavored water ices; and in the seventeenth century, the Italians made the first ice cream, using ice from the hills. It wasn't until the 1830s, however, when the first icemaking machines were invented, that preserving food by freezing it became a practical possibility.

"To make cream ice. Peel, stone and scald twelve apricots, beat them fine in a mortar, and put to them six ounces of sugar and a pint of scalding cream. Work it through a fine sieve, put it into a tin that hath a close cover, and set it in a tub of ice broken small and a large quantity of salt put among it. When you see your cream grow thick around the edges, stir it and set it in again until it is all frozen up. Then put on the lid and have ready another tub with ice and salt as before: put your tin in the middle and lay ice over and under it: let it stand four or five hours, and then dip your tin in warm water before you turn it out. You may use any sort of fruit if you have not apricots, only observe to work it fine."

From THE EXPERIENCED ENGLISH HOUSEKEEPER
by ELIZABETH RAFFALD, 1769

MEAT

Nowadays the butcher does all the work for us and we buy our meat ready to cook, but in the old days it would be hung in the larder for a period before eating in order to tenderize the fibers.

FRESH UNCOOKED MEAT
As soon as you get this home, remove it from its wrapping and wipe with a clean, damp cloth. Store in the refrigerator covered with wax paper.

COOKED MEAT
Remove the meat from its wrapping paper and store in the refrigerator, either in the meat compartment or in a refrigerator bag.

MUTTON FOR BOILING
Mutton for boiling is usually leg, neck, or breast. These cuts should not be allowed to hang for too many days, as any taint will spoil the flavor of the finished dish.

FISH

Oily fish should be eaten as fresh as possible. Turbot, brill, and halibut will keep in a cool place for a day or two. A whole fish is best kept hung up by the tail.

POULTRY & GAME BIRDS

After killing, poultry and game should be hung for a while, like meat, head downwards, in a cool, airy place. Chicken should be hung for 24 hours, geese and ducks for one or two days, turkeys for three to five days, and older birds for a few days longer.

Freshly killed game birds, such as pheasant and grouse, need to be hung for longer – from about seven to ten days, or until the breast feathers are easily plucked out.

MILK & CREAM

TO KEEP MILK

Pour milk into a jug, then stand the jug in a basin of cold water and cover with a thick cloth, with the ends in the water. Add a pinch of bicarbonate of soda to prevent milk going sour quickly. Keep milk covered tightly, as it quickly absorbs odors from other foods.

TO KEEP MILK AND CREAM

Pour the milk or cream into a container, and leave to stand in boiling water until the surface looks thick and creamy (it shouldn't get so hot that it boils, however). Remove it from the water and transfer to a cool place. Fresh cream treated this way should keep for 24 hours.

MONGOLIAN DRIED MILK

The idea of drying milk to make it keep is nothing new – Mongolian nomads were doing this at the time of Marco Polo. The first stage in the process was to bring the milk to just below boiling point. Then, when the cream had risen to the surface, they would skim it off and set it aside to be made into butter. As long as the milk contained fat, it could not be dried, so the final stage was to stand the milk in the sun to dry.

When the time came to go on an expedition, the nomads would take with them about 10 lb of this dried milk. Every morning, during the course of their journey, they would take out about half a pound of it and place it, with as much water as they liked, in a gourd-shaped leather flask. The motion of their riding would mix together the water and the milk, and the rehydrated milk would serve as their breakfast.

KEEPING BUTTER COOL

Before the days of the refrigerator, butter could be kept in special butter coolers made of red brick. These had a bell-shaped cover, and cold water could be poured over the cover to keep the butter cool.

You can, in fact, easily make a cooler of your own. Place the butter on a plate, cover with a flowerpot, and put this into a deep dish containing ¼ oz saltpeter to 1 quart cold water. Arrange a piece of muslin or blanket over the flowerpot, with the ends just dipping into the liquid.

Another method is to knead the butter in cold water to extract the buttermilk, then place in a glazed jar. Turn this upside-down inside another, and fill with sufficient cold water to exclude the air, renewing the water every day.

KEEPING CHEESE FRESH

In order to keep cheese fresh, wrap it in a cloth dampened with vinegar and store it in a cool place (but not in the refrigerator).

"If you will have a very dainty Nettle Cheese, which is the finest Summer Cheese which can be eaten…as soon as it is drained from the brine, you shall lay it upon fresh Nettles, and cover it all over with the same, and let it ripen therein. Observing to renew your Nettles once in two days, and every time you renew them, to turn the Cheese. Gather your Nettles as much without stalks as may be, and make the bed both under and aloft as smooth as may be: for the fewer wrinkles your Cheese hath, the more dainty is your House-wife accounted."
From THE ENGLISH HOUSEWIFE, 1683

EGGS

"A supply of fresh unwashed eggs should be secured in the spring, when they are cheap, and preserved either in water glass, which is the cleanest and least trouble, or in cold, fresh slaked limewater. You can then . . . use them for cooking purposes all through the following winter instead of fresh eggs, which are so dear."

From AN EARLY TWENTIETH-CENTURY COOKERY BOOK

TO KEEP EGGS FRESH

- Rub them with butter, sweet oil, or melted lard to close the pores, then pack them in bran or sawdust, without allowing them to touch each other.
- Place them for a minute in nearly boiling water, and they will keep for a month.
- Place them in a sieve, lower it into boiling water, boil the eggs for 20 seconds, and store them in sawdust: they will keep for two or three months.
- Steep them for a little while in sweet oil, and they will keep for six months.

TO KEEP YOLKS

Beat the yolk with a little cold water, and it will keep fresh for several days.

Alternatively, place the yolk in a narrow or tall glass container and cover with milk or water, then cover the container and store it in the fridge.

TO KEEP THE WHITES

Place them in a glass jar, cover with a lid, and store in the refrigerator.

STORING FRUIT & VEGETABLES

Do not store carrots next to apples, or they will take on a bitter taste. Keep potatoes and onions apart, as potatoes stored with onions will quickly spoil. Before storing root vegetables, cut off the leaves to prevent the sap rising and so drying out the roots.

TO KEEP CABBAGES
Cut the cabbages at the base so that they have about 2 inches of stem left below the leaves. Using a small knife, scoop out the pith inside as far as you can. Tie a cord around the cabbages and hang them upside-down. Every day, fill the scooped-out hollows with water, and the cabbages will stay fresh.

TO PRESERVE POLE BEANS
Wipe the beans with a clean cloth, and remove the strings. The beans may now be sliced or left whole, as you prefer. Place them in layers in a jar, with plenty of dry salt between each layer, finishing with a good layer of salt on the top. Cover with a plate, and place a weight on top, such as a brick or stone. Before using them, soak them in cold water for 12 hours.

TO KEEP CELERY
If you have any odd pieces left over, these may be dried in a slow oven. The dried celery will keep for weeks, and can be used in soups and stews.

APPLES

Discard any fruit that is bruised or damaged by wasps. Wrap each apple in newspaper or oiled paper, and store in a cool, dark, airy place. To keep the air moist, sprinkle the floor with water from time to time.

PEARS

Pears should be wrapped for storage like apples. A day or two before they are to be eaten, bring them into a warm room: this improves their flavor.

QUINCES

Quinces should be stored like pears, but it is important to keep them away from other fruit:

"Now for Quinces, they are a fruit which by no means you may place near any other kind of fruit, because their scent is so strong and piercing, that it will enter into any fruit and clean take away his natural relish. The time of their gathering is ever in October: and the meetest place to lie them in is where they may have most air and lie dry (for wet they can by no means endure): also they must not lie close, because the smell of them is both strong and unwholesome."

From THE ENGLISH HUSBANDMAN, 1635

KEEPING LEMONS & LIMES FRESH

- To keep lemons fresh, place them in a glass jar, fill it with water, and cover tightly.
- To keep limes fresh, place them in a jar, cover, and store in the refrigerator.

KEEPING CUT FRUIT FRESH

Cover the exposed part of the fruit with waxed paper, and place fruit, cut side down, on a dish – or you can simply cover the fruit with a glass.

JAMS, JELLIES, & PRESERVES

Apart from baking your own bread, what could conjure up the atmosphere and aromas of the old-fashioned kitchen more than making your own jams or preserves? These can be made either from fruit from your own garden or from wild berries.

When making jams or preserves, the cooks of old knew the importance of having the freshest ingredients and always followed the golden rule "one hour from the garden to the pot."

"The rule is, jam to-morrow and jam yesterday – but never jam to-day."

From ALICE THROUGH THE LOOKING-GLASS by LEWIS CARROLL (1832-98)

GETTING JAM TO SET

Getting a good "set" depends on the presence of three things – pectin and acid (both natural substances found in fruit) and sugar. The acid helps to release the pectin, and the pectin works with the sugar to form a gel and set the jam.

Some fruits, including apples, damsons, gooseberries, and blackcurrants, are rich in pectin. Others (strawberries, cherries, and rhubarb, for example) contain no pectin and need help to set.

ECONOMY JAM

To every pound of fruit pulp, add only ¾ lb loaf sugar, substituting 1 teaspoon of glycerine for the remaining sugar. Jam made in this way will be cheaper, clearer, and will last indefinitely.

THE PECTIN TEST

To test whether fruit contains sufficient pectin to set well, place 1 teaspoon of unsweetened cooked fruit pulp in a glass jar, and leave to cool. Add 3 teaspoons of methylated spirits to the jar, cover with the lid, and shake gently. If a large clot forms, the fruit has enough pectin; if there are a number of small clots, the pectin content is too low. This can be remedied by adding 2 tablespoons of lemon juice to every 4 lb of fruit.

TESTING THE SET

Place a teaspoonful of jam on a cold saucer (chill one in advance in your refrigerator). A skin will form as the jam cools. Push the skin lightly with your finger. If it crinkles, the jam has reached setting point.

Another way to test the set is to stir the jam with a wooden spoon and allow some to cool in the bowl of the spoon. Then drop it from the spoon: if the jam has partly set, and falls off the spoon in large flakes rather than drops, it is ready.

"To preserve Damsons. Take Damsons before they be full ripe, but gathered off the Tree. Allow to every pound of them a pound of Sugar, put a little Rose-water to them, and set them in the bottom of your pan one by one. Boil them with a soft fire, and as they seeth strew your Sugar upon them, and let them boil till the Syrup be thick. Then while the Syrup is yet warm, take the Damsons out and put them into a covered gally pot, Syrup and all."

From A BOOK OF FRUITS AND FLOWERS by THOMAS JENNER, 1653

PRESERVING FRUIT IN BRANDY

English country housewives suggest this delicious way of preserving berry fruit. The preserve is said to keep for years, if not eaten sooner.

Place 1 lb small firm strawberries in a large stone jar, add 1 lb loaf sugar, and pour a bottle of good brandy over the fruit to cover it. Cover the jar with a double layer of greaseproof paper tied round with string, then place a tight-fitting lid on the jar.

When raspberries are ripe, open the jar and stir the mixture. Then add 1 lb of raspberries and 1 lb of loaf sugar, and cover as before. Follow the raspberries with cherries. These should be stoned, but add the kernals.

Continue with other fruits, avoiding any that are seedy or pippy, up to maximum of 5 lb.

The preserve should be served in wine glasses, accompanied by sponge fingers.

HOW TO BOTTLE JAM

Jam must be tightly sealed if it is to keep well. ensure that the cover fits properly:

- Wet cellophane jam-pot covers before putting them on the jars, and they will contract as they dry.
- Cover with greaseproof paper dipped in egg white.
- Cover with tissue paper dipped in milk.

To open jars easily, place them upside down in hot water for a few minutes.

COVERING JELLY JARS WITH WAX

Pour a thin layer of paraffin wax on top of the jelly; then place a strong piece of string on top of it, with one end hanging over the edge of the glass, and pour on another layer of wax. Then, when the jelly is to be used, the wax can easily be removed with the string.

TIME TO PICKLE

Pickling is a way of preserving vegetables in vinegar, usually adding spices for flavor.

According to country lore, red cabbage, cauliflower, peppers, chilies, cucumbers, shallots, garlic, gherkins, melons, mushrooms for ketchup, nasturtiums, onions, tomatoes, and globe artichokes should all be pickled in August.

If you are pickling onions with white vinegar, add a few drops of sweet oil of almonds to each jar to keep the onions white.

"To Pickle Cucumbers for the winter-time. Put them in an earthenware vessel: lay first a lay of salt and Dill, then a lay of Cucumbers, and so till they be all laid. Put in some Mace and whole Peppers, and some Fennel-Seed: then fill it up with Malt or Beer-vinegar: and put a clean board and a stone upon it to . . . keep them close covered."

From THE COMPLEAT COOK, 1671

WHEN TO DRY HERBS

According to country wisdom, August is the time to dry parsley, thyme, lavender, rosemary, marjoram, basil, balm, burnet, savory, tarragon, and sage.

"Of leaves, choose only such as are green, and full of juice, and cast away such as are any way declining, for they will putrefy the rest. Dry them well in the sun (and not in the shade, as the saying of physicians is): for if the Sun draw away the virtues of the herb, it must needs do the like by hay ... which the experience of every country farmer will explode for a notable piece of nonsense. Having well dried them, put them up in brown paper, sewing the paper up like a sack, and press them not too hard together, and keep them in a dry place near the fire."

From the ENGLISH PHYSICIAN by NICHOLAS CULPEPER, 1653

CANDIED FLOWERS

"To Candy all kind of Flowers as they grow, with their stalks on. Take the Flowers and cut the stalk somewhat short: then take one pound of the whitest and hardest Sugar, put to it eight spoons of Rosewater, and boil it till it will roll between your finger and your thumb. Then take it from the fire, and as it waxeth cold dip in all your Flowers: and taking them out suddenly, lay them one by one in the bottom of a sieve. Then turn a stool with the feet upwards, set the sieve on the feet, cover it with a fair linen cloth, and set a chafing-dish of coals in the midst of the stool and underneath the sieve: the heat thereof will dry your Candy presently. Then box them up, and they will keep all the year, and look very pleasantly."

From A BOOK OF FRUITS AND FLOWERS by THOMAS JENNER, 1653

TO KEEP PARSLEY FRESH

Wash thoroughly, shake off the excess water, place in a glass jar, cover, and keep in the refrigerator.

COOKED TWICE

The word "biscuit" comes from the French *bis cuit*, meaning "twice cooked." This double cooking was a way of preserving the small hard cakes taken on board ship as part of the crew's diet. The cakes had to be cooked on land first, or they would have gone moldy on long sea voyages. Before eating them, the sailors had the cakes cooked again so they would be crisp.

HOW TO KEEP LEFTOVER PASTRY

If there is sufficient pastry left over after baking, wrap it up in a damp piece of muslin or cheesecloth. Wrap this in another, dry cloth. Pastry keeps best if it has a high fat content and does not contain baking powder.

KEEPING LEFTOVER PIMIENTOS

To keep leftover canned pimientos, place them in a small dish and cover with cooking oil.

TO KEEP YEAST

Fresh yeast will keep for a week if it is placed in a small basin and covered with water.

CHAPTER THREE

IN THE KITCHEN

A BAD WORKMAN ALWAYS BLAMES HIS TOOLS, or so the old saying goes, and this is as true of cookery as of any other practical art. In fact, the cook's time in the kitchen is both more productive and more pleasurable if backed by a sound knowledge of cooking techniques and by good kitchen practices.

"He is an ill cook that cannot lick his own fingers."
TRADITIONAL SAYINGS

THE OPEN FIRE

Roasting meat over a fire – which survives in the modern barbecue and spit roasting – was probably the earliest method of cooking. According to the poet Homer, the ancient Greek heroes were no strangers to the pleasures of the barbecue. Homer describes how Achilles entertained Odysseus outside the walls of the great city of Troy. Achilles' companions first helped him to carve up a sheep, a goat, and part of a wild hog. The fire was then made to blaze up, and when the flames had died down the embers were scattered. Spits to hold the meat were arranged on logs over the fire, and the meat was sprinkled with salt. When it was cooked, Achilles and the others served it to their guest, with bread, in "handsome baskets."

FRUITFUL KINDLING

The dried pith of lemons and oranges may be used as kindling to start a fire.

FIRE WITHOUT SMOKE

If you are having a picnic in a place where fires are prohibited, here is a way to barbecue meat without either fire or smoke. Put a few pieces of unslaked lime into a flat tin box and add a little water. Place a steak on top of the lid, and it will soon be cooked.

IN THE POT

Boiling food in water was more difficult than roasting it over a fire, because a container was needed to hold the water. Over the centuries, people have come up with all kinds of ingenious solutions.

One very early solution was to make a hollow in the earth, and line it with stones to make it waterproof. Other stones would then be heated in the fire, and transferred to the water to bring it to the boil.

Large mollusc or reptile shells were another early "pot." These were still being used in the Amazon region in the nineteenth century; here a soup called *sarapatel* made of chopped turtle entrails was boiled in the upper shell of the animal.

In Indonesia, a technique still used in recent times was to cook food in a hollow piece of bamboo. One end would be sealed with clay, little pieces of meat and some liquid would be inserted, and the other end of the cane stopped with more clay.

But perhaps the cleverest solution of all was to let the animal provide its own cooking pot. The ancient nomadic peoples of the Near East had this method down to a fine art. First the animal would be carved up, and then the bones would be placed on the fire, where they would burn away merrily. The meat would be placed in the large stomach bag, with some water, and this would be suspended over the fire. In this way, the animal literally cooked itself.

"Youk'n hide de fier, but w'at you gwine do wid de smoke?"

From UNCLE REMUS : LEGENDS OF THE OLD PLANTATION by JOEL CHANDLER HARRIS (1848-1908)

HAM IN HAY

In French farmhouses, the traditional way of cooking ham was to enclose it in hay. The meat was wrapped in a cloth and placed on a bed of sweet hay. It would then be surrounded with more hay, covered with water, and boiled. The hay gave the ham a particularly fragrant flavor.

"There's nothing like eating hay when you're faint."
"I didn't say there was nothing better," the King replied,
"I said there was nothing like it."

From ALICE THROUGH THE LOOKING-GLASS
by LEWIS CARROLL (1832-98)

POTATOES IN CLAY

An unglazed, earthenware pot called a *diable* is used in France to cook potatoes. The potatoes are scrubbed but not peeled, and, while they cook, the clay absorbs some of their moisture and gives them a wonderful, earthy flavor.

COOKING OVER VINE CUTTINGS

In the wine-producing districts of France food is often grilled over vine cuttings, which gives it a delightfully aromatic taste.

HOW NOT TO BOIL EGGS

Do not place the eggs in boiling water. Hard-boiled eggs cooked from the start in boiling water are likely to be tough and leathery, and soft-boiled eggs tend to be unevenly cooked.

SIX WAYS TO BOIL EGGS

METHOD 1
Place eggs in a saucepan, cover with cold water and heat slowly to boiling. For soft-boiled eggs, remove when the water starts to boil. For hard-boiled eggs, reduce heat and simmer for 5 to 8 minutes.

METHOD 2
Bring a large saucepan of water to the boil. Take it off the heat, and add the eggs. Cover the pan and replace it on the heat. Allow 3 minutes from the moment the water boils again. Larger eggs may need a further minute's cooking off the heat.

METHOD 3
Pour hot water into both sections of a double boiler. When the water in the lower part boils, place eggs in the top. Cook soft-boiled eggs for 12 to 15 minutes, hard-boiled ones for 25 to 30 minutes. The advantage of this method is that the temperature of the eggs does not reach boiling point, so they cook evenly.

METHOD 4
Using ¾ pint of water for every two eggs, bring the water to the boil in a fairly deep pan. Remove from the heat and lower the eggs into the water, cover, then cook for 4 minutes without letting the water boil.

METHOD 5
Boil the water, then put in the eggs. Remove from the heat and cover. Leave the eggs in the water 6 minutes for soft-boiled eggs, 25 minutes for hard-boiled.

METHOD 6
Plunge the eggs into a pan of boiling water, and cover. Leave on the heat for 1 minute, then remove and leave for a further 5 minutes.

"An egg boiled soft is not unwholesome."
From EMMA by JANE AUSTEN (1775-1815)

HOW TO POACH AN EGG

Really new-laid eggs have whites which fly around too much during poaching, while the whites of older eggs go rubbery. The best eggs for poaching are two or three days old.

METHOD *1*
Dip each egg into a saucepan of boiling water for exactly 30 seconds. This slightly cooks the outer layer, so that the egg will keep more intact during poaching. Place another pan of water on the heat to boil, adding a few drops of vinegar, then break the egg into a saucer. When the water is boiling, swirl it around with a wooden spoon to make a whirlpool in the center, and slide in the egg, continuing to swirl the water until it boils again. Remove from the heat, cover the pan, and leave for nearly 3 minutes.

METHOD *2*
This method allows you to cook two eggs at once. Bring a pan of water to the boil and break the eggs into a saucer. When the water is just about to boil, slide in the eggs. As the white starts to set, quickly turn the eggs over a couple of times with a metal spoon, so that they form a nice oval shape, with the yolk in the middle. Remove from the heat, cover the pan, and leave for nearly 15 minutes.

ROAST EGGS

There's an old saying "I have eggs on the spit," meaning "I am too busy to attend to anything else." Eggs were indeed once roasted on spits – and no doubt needed constant watching.

The eggs were first boiled, then the yolks were removed, mixed with aromatic spices, and put back into the eggs. The eggs would then be threaded onto a spit and roasted.

> *"One likes the pheasant's wing, and one the leg;*
> *The vulgar boil, the learned roast an egg."*
> ALEXANDER POPE (1688-1744)

TESTING OVEN HEAT WITH FLOUR

To test the temperature of your oven, sprinkle a little flour in a pan and place it in the heated oven.

- If the flour turns a delicate brown in 5 minutes, the oven temperature is low (250-325°F).
- If the flour turns golden brown in 5 minutes, the oven temperature is moderate (325-400°F).
- If the flour turns deep brown in 5 minutes, the oven temperature is hot (400-450°F).
- If the flour turns a deep, dark brown in 3 minutes, the oven temperature is very hot (450-500°F).

TESTING OVEN HEAT WITH PAPER

Instead of flour, you can use a piece of writing paper to test the temperature of your oven. Simply place the paper in the heated oven.

- If the paper burns, the oven is too hot for cooking.
- If the paper turns dark brown, the temperature is right for pastry, scones, muffins, and rolls.
- If the paper turns light brown, the temperature is right for small cakes, pies, and tarts.
- If the paper turns dark yellow, the temperature is right for cakes.
- If the paper turns light yellow, the temperature is right for cookies and baked puddings.

TESTING THE HEAT OF FRYING FAT WITH BREAD

You can test the temperature of fat used for frying by browning a 1 inch cube of bread.

- If the cube browns in 60 seconds, the temperature will be 350-365°F – right for frying dry uncooked foods such as doughnuts and fritters.
- If the cube browns in 40 seconds, the temperature will be 365-382°F – right for frying such foods as cheese balls, croquettes, fish, and oysters.
- If the cube browns in 20 seconds, the temperature will be 382-390°F – right for frying wet uncooked foods such as French fries and potato balls.

"Water boils when it gallops, oil when it stands still."
MRS BEETON, 1914

TESTING THE HEAT OF A GRIDDLE WITH WATER

Place a few drops of water on the griddle. If the water scatters, the griddle is hot enough for cooking.

SHEET IRON TO SAVE FUEL

If you have a gas hob, you can economize on fuel by placing a piece of sheet iron, about 10 or 12 inches square, over one of the rings. When the sheet is hot, it will keep three or four saucepans boiling at the same time – but make sure that it doesn't tip up and take care you don't burn yourself on it.

TEMPERATURES FOR CANDY & FROSTINGS

If you don't have a sugar thermometer to test whether a frosting or candy has reached the right stage, there are some old-fashioned alternatives.

SYRUP
This has reached the thread stage (228-234°F) if it spins a 2 inch thread when dropped from a spoon.

FUDGE, FROSTING, FONDANT
These have reached the soft-ball stage (234-240°F) when a small amount dropped into cold water forms a soft ball, which flattens when removed.

CARAMEL
This has reached the firm-ball stage (244-248°F) when a small amount dropped into cold water forms a firm ball and does not flatten when removed.

DIVINITY, NOUGAT, POPCORN BALLS, AND SALT-WATER TAFFY
These have reached the hard-ball stage (250-265°F) when a small amount dropped into cold water forms a ball that holds its shape.

BUTTERSCOTCH TAFFY AND PULLED CANDIES
These have reached the crack stage (270-290°F) when a small amount dropped into cold water separates into threads, but is not brittle.

BRITTLE GLACÉ FOR NUTS AND FRUITS
This has reached the hard-crack stage (295-310°F) when a small amount dropped into cold water separates into hard, brittle threads.

CARAMEL BURNT SUGAR
This has reached the right temperature (310°F) when the clear to brown liquid becomes hard when cool.

PREPARING CAKE PANS

One way to prepare a cake pan is to mix ½ cup of shortening and ¼ cup of flour to a smooth paste. Spread thinly on the pan. Keep a supply of the mixture in a covered dish to use when needed.

Suet is the best kind of fat for greasing cake pans. If you use suet, the cakes will not burn so readily, and will come out more easily.

Instead of greasing cake pans, you can line them with plain or waxed paper. Cut several pieces at a time to fit the bottom of pans, and keep them on hand.

TO TEST WHEN A CAKE IS COOKED

You can tell when a cake is baked if:

- A cake tester or toothpick inserted into the center comes out clean.
- The cake shrinks from the edges of the pan.
- The cake springs back when touched lightly with the finger (small cakes and cookies are ready if they spring back and are brown).

To remove pie, cake, or bread pans from the oven, use a large pancake-turner or a pair of strong tongs.

Marbles

USE YOUR MARBLES

If you place a marble in milk, sauces, custards, and stews, you don't have to stir them so often and it helps prevent burning.

To prevent "furring," keep a marble in your kettle.

PREVENTING STICKING & BURNING

MILK, CUSTARD, RICE, MACARONI
Grease the bottom of the pan with butter before adding any of these ingredients.

PASTA
Place the pasta in a colander or sieve and lower into the boiling water.

CHOCOLATE
Grease all around the inside of the container in which you are going to melt chocolate. The chocolate won't stick, and so less will be wasted.

Another way to melt chocolate without burning is to place it on waxed paper in the top of a double boiler, and heat until melted.

PREVENTING SPLASHES WHEN FRYING

WHEN FRYING FISH OR MEAT
Sprinkle a little salt in the frying pan before adding the fat or oil. This will not only prevent splashing, but will also help the flavor of the food.

WHEN FRYING EGGS
Sprinkle a little flour into the fat or oil. This will also help the eggs to brown.

PREVENTING POTS BOILING OVER

To prevent milk, custard, rice, or macaroni from boiling over, grease the top inch of the pan lightly with butter.

Add 1 tablespoon of cooking oil or shortening to the water to prevent pasta boiling over.

WASHING KITCHEN UTENSILS

Washing up becomes much easier if you soak utensils immediately after using them, so that food left on them does not get a chance to harden. The only utensils that should not be soaked are those made of wood or ones with glued handles.

ALUMINUM
Wash aluminum pans with soap and water, and scour to remove any spots. Dry thoroughly after washing.

CHROME
Wash with soap and water. Polish with a soft cloth.

COPPER
Lacquered copper should be washed with soap and water, and then dried thoroughly. Unlacquered copper should first be polished with copper polish, then washed and dried.

GLASS AND ENAMEL
Wash in soap and water, and rub any stubborn marks with scouring pads or a fine cleansing powder. Do this gently on enamel, so you do not scratch the surface.

IRON
Iron pans should be washed with soap and water, but shouldn't be scoured. It is particularly important to dry them thoroughly, in order to prevent rusting.

STEEL
Wash with soap and water, scour to remove spots, then rinse and dry.

TIN
Wash and scour, if necessary, with a mild cleansing powder. Like iron, tin rusts easily, so must always be dried thoroughly.

WOOD
Scrape wooden utensils with a blunt blade, then wash in lukewarm water.

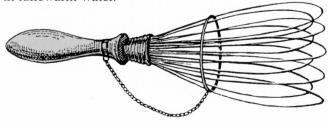

CLEANING A FRYING PAN WITH BREAD

"Do not scrub the inside of your frying pans, unless they be of enamelled iron, as, after this operation, any preparation fried is liable to catch or burn in the pan. If the pan has become black inside, rub it with a hard crust of bread, and wash in hot water, mixed with a little soda."

From MRS BEETON'S
COOKERY BOOK, 1914

*"I had a little doll, the prettiest ever seen,
She washed me the dishes, and kept the house clean."*

NURSERY RHYME

DOING THE WASHING UP

"Clear as you go: muddle makes more muddle."
*"Not to wash plates and dishes soon after using
makes work."*
*"Dirty saucepans filled with hot water begin
to clean themselves."*
"Do not throw anything but water down the sink."
"Never put the handles of knives in hot water."
*"When washing-up is over
for the day, wash the tea-cloth; it saves the cloths
and cleanses the hands."*

KITCHEN MAXIMS QUOTED BY MRS BEETON, 1914

TEA-CLOTH Dishcloth.

TIPS ON CLEANING & CARE

BURNT AND GREASY PANS
To make a blackened or greasy pan easier to clean, fill it with 1 inch of water, and add a teaspoon of washing soda (sal soda). Cover and heat to boiling.

THE TEAPOT
Any stains on the inside can be removed with a mild scouring powder; the teapot should then be washed with hot, soapy water, rinsed with boiling water, drained, and dried. To avoid staining, do not leave tea in the pot for any length of time.

THE COFFEEPOT
Clean in the same way as the teapot. Alternatively, you can boil a solution of baking soda and water in the pot for 5 minutes, then rinse in boiling water.

Cloth filters should be washed in a solution of baking soda and water, and rinsed well. Keep filters that you use each day in a covered glass of cold water. New filters should be rinsed thoroughly in cold water before you use them.

THE KETTLE
The inside of kettles often becomes caked with lime deposit. To remove this, fill the kettle with equal parts of water and vinegar and heat to boiling. Leave the water to stand for several hours, and you should then be able to scrape off the deposit.

Polly put the kettle on,
Polly put the kettle on,
Polly put the kettle on,
We'll all have tea.
TRADITIONAL SONG

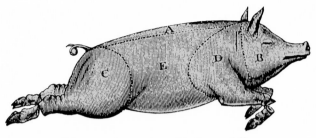

The sow came in with the saddle,
The little pig rocked the cradle,
The dish jumped up on the table,
To see the pot swallow the ladle.
The spit that stood behind the door
Threw the pudding-stick on the floor.
Odd's-bobs! says the gridiron,
Can't you agree?
I'm the head constable,
Bring them to me.

TRADITIONAL RHYME

THE WAFFLE IRON
Use a small, stiff brush to get into all the crevices in the waffle iron.

THE EGG BEATER
Wash the beater in cold water first to remove any food particles, then wash with the other utensils and dishes. Never immerse the cogs in water. The beaters on an electric beater should be removed for washing so that no water gets into the motor.

THE FOOD PROCESSOR
Take the processor apart and wash the individual parts thoroughly. Dry well before reassembling.

If you don't use the appliance regularly, rub the parts that come into contact with food with unsalted fat and store in a paper bag. Wipe the fat off before using.

To prevent dried fruits from clogging the blade, add a few drops of lemon juice before grinding.

THE FLOUR SIFTER
Keep the sifter in the flour bin, a paper sack, or any other kind of container, so that it stays dry and free of dust and grease, and is ready to use when required.

REMOVING STAINS

FROM ALUMINUM PANS
Place some rotten apples in the pan, cover with water, bring to the boil, and the stains will disappear.

FROM THE HANDS
To remove vegetable or fruit stains from the hands:
- Rub them with a slice of lemon.
- Rub them with a crust of bread dipped in vinegar.
- Grease your hands with lard, then wash them with soap and water.

REMOVING ODORS

FROM JARS AND BOTTLES
Pour a solution of water and dry mustard into them and let them stand for several hours. Alternatively, use a dilute chlorine solution, then rinse in hot water.

WHEN COOKING FISH
Cover the fish with browned butter or lemon juice. To remove fish odors from cooking utensils, add 2 tablespoons of ammonia to the washing-up water.

WHEN BOILING MEAT
Add a piece of charcoal to the water when boiling ham and other meats to help prevent smells.

ONIONS AND CABBAGE
To prevent smells when cooking onions or cabbage, add 1 tablespoon of lemon juice or a wedge of lemon with the skin on. Adding charcoal to the water also prevents smells when boiling onions or cabbage.

In order to remove the smell of onions from your hands, wash them in cold water. Also, use cold water to wash the knife used for cutting. After eating onions, take half a teaspoon of salt.

*"Thrust an oniony knife into the earth
to take away the smell."*

MRS BEETON, 1914

CHAPTER FOUR

THE SECRETS OF THE COOK

E VEN THE MOST EXPERIENCED COOK
is sometimes confronted with disaster:
the mayonnaise curdles, the crisp lettuce of a day
ago looks limp, and you haven't got enough eggs for
the cake that you're planning to bake. This is where
the secrets handed down from cook to cook can
come to the rescue and save the day.

*"A spoilt dinner will spoil a good temper and
disarrange a whole household."*
TRADITIONAL SAYING

THE CHARACTER OF THE COOK

While the ingredients are of paramount importance, the character and habits of the cook also play a crucial role in the success of any dish:

"The Cook must be cleanly both in body and garments. She must have a quick eye, a curious nose, a perfect taste, and a ready ear; and she must not be butter-fingered, sweet-toothed, nor faint-hearted. For the first will let everything fall; the second will consume what it should increase; and the last will lose time with too much niceness."

From THE ENGLISH HOUSEWIFE, 1683

MEAT & SAUSAGES

TO FLOUR MEAT OR CHICKEN

If you need to flour a piece of meat or poultry, try this simple but effective method. Place the meat in a paper bag with the flour and shake well. The result will be a fine, even coating without any lumps.

TO PREVENT BACON CURLING

The thinner a slice of bacon, the more likely it is to curl up at the edges during cooking. For evenly cooked, flat bacon, snip the edges with kitchen shears before cooking, or broil between racks.

HANDLING SMALL PIECES OF MEAT

If you have to prepare small pieces of meat, threading them onto skewers while you work makes them much easier to handle.

TO PREVENT TIPS OF CROWN ROAST BURNING

Crown roast is an impressive dish, but the effect can be somewhat spoiled if the tips of the "crown" become burned. To avoid this, place the roast in a pan with the bones downwards, or spear the tips with pieces of fat meat.

TO SKIN SAUSAGES

Immerse sausages in cold water for a minute and they become easier to skin.

TO PREVENT SAUSAGES BURSTING

To maintain the shape of sausages, so that they come out of the pan smooth-skinned and evenly browned, dip them in boiling water before frying.

PLUCKING POULTRY & GAME BIRDS

Poultry should ideally be plucked soon after killing, for the bird will still be warm and the feathers easier to remove. Game birds are best plucked after hanging.

To pluck a bird, hold it firmly on a large sheet of paper. Begin by plucking out the feathers at the top of the breast, taking two to three at a time and pulling them downwards towards the bird's head. Use a lighted taper to singe off the down and hairs, then wipe the bird clean.

To make plucking quicker, and also cleaner, plunge the bird for four or five minutes into boiling water. Not only does this make it easier to pull the feathers out, but it also stops them flying about, and kills any insects that may be on the bird.

FISH

HOW LONG TO COOK
Fish is a delicate food, and so should be cooked for a short time and at a gentle heat. Cooking it for a long time, and at a high temperature, will make it tough and spoil the flavor.

A GOLDEN COATING
For a rich yellow coating on fish that is to be fried, use semolina instead of breadcrumbs.

TO KEEP FISH WHOLE
When poaching fish, you may find some of it gets lost because the flesh disintegrates into the water. To keep your fish intact, wrap it loosely in a piece of muslin or cheesecloth before lowering it into the water. It can then be lifted out whole when cooking is complete.

TO MAKE BOILED FISH FIRM AND WHITE
To preserve the color and texture of boiled fish, add a little lemon juice to the water while boiling.

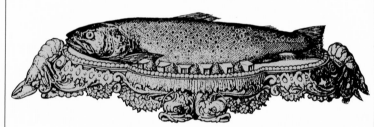

"Fish must swim thrice – once in the water, a second time in the sauce, and a third time in wine in the stomach."

TRADITIONAL FRENCH SAYING

REMOVING CREEPY-CRAWLIES FROM VEGETABLES

"Have vegetables gathered from the garden at an early hour, so that there is ample time to search for caterpillars, etc. These disagreeable additions need never make their appearance on table in cauliflowers or cabbages, if the vegetable in its raw state is allowed to soak in salt and water for an hour or so."

From MRS BEETON'S COOKERY BOOK, 1914

PREPARING VEGETABLES

SCRUBBING NEW POTATOES
- Before scrubbing the potatoes, soak them in salted water for about half an hour.
- Place the potatoes in a basin, cover with boiling water, and leave to soak.
- If they have just come out of the ground, all you need do is rub the potatoes with a coarse towel.

PEELING ONIONS
A trick to stop onions bringing tears to your eyes is to peel them under water.

TO PEEL CARROTS
Drop the carrots into boiling water and leave them to stand for a few minutes before paring off the skin.

SKINNING TOMATOES
- Push a fork into the stem end, then plunge the tomato into boiling water and then into cold water
- Leave the tomatoes in boiling water to soak for a few minutes.
- Hold the tomatoes over direct heat. When the skin has loosened, break it at the stem end, and peel the skin back.

CLEANING LEEKS AND CELERY
Leeks and celery can be full of soil and grit, inaccessibly hidden in the layers and stubbornly refusing to come out. To flush out this dirt, place the vegetables, with green ends down, in a deep jug of water. Most of the soil and grit will then fall out. When the vegetables are split, all they will need is a final rinse.

TO DRAW OUT EXCESS WATER OR BITTER JUICES
Marrows, cucumbers, and tomatoes contain a large amount of water, which can make them taste insipid. Eggplants, too, may contain bitter juices that will spoil their flavor. To remove excess water or juices, cut the vegetables into slices and sprinkle salt over the cut surfaces. Place in a colander or on a flat dish to drain for an hour or two.

TO EXTRACT FROST FROM POTATOES AND GREENS
After peeling, leave the vegetables to soak in cold water for an hour. Boil them with a small piece of saltpeter, and this will remove the sweet taste caused by the frost.

COOKING VEGETABLES

HOW LONG TO COOK
Stem vegetables should be cooked quickly, root vegetables slowly.

FLAVORFUL POTATOES
To retain their full flavor, potatoes are best cooked in their skins. They can then be peeled, if liked.

SOFT-SKINNED POTATOES
To keep the skins of baked potatoes soft and tender to eat, grease them before baking.

QUICK-COOK BEETROOT
If beetroots are very large, you can cut them in half to reduce the cooking time – but remember to singe the cut parts with a red-hot poker first to prevent the color "bleeding" out.

KEEPING VEGETABLES HOT
Before the days of heated trolleys and electric hotplates, cooks had to rely on simpler methods in order to keep the vegetables hot while the rest of the meal was being assembled.

To keep root vegetables hot, place them in hot vegetable dishes and stand the dishes, with the lids on, on top of a pan of boiling water.

Place leaf vegetables in a colander and press them to remove all water. Then stand the colander, uncovered, over a pan of boiling water. When it is time to serve the vegetables, they should be pressed again, then transferred to a vegetable dish and covered.

Hokey, pokey, whisky, thum,
How d'you like potatoes done?
Boiled in whisky, boiled in rum,
Says the King of the Cannibal Islands.
NINETEENTH-CENTURY JINGLE

RETAINING NATURAL COLOR

POTATOES, SWEET POTATOES, AND APPLES
To stop potatoes, sweet potatoes, and apples going brown, place them in salted water immediately after paring off the skin.

TO KEEP LEAF VEGETABLES GREEN
Add a little baking soda to the water in which the vegetables are boiled.

TO KEEP BEETROOT RED
To prevent beetroot bleeding, dip the pieces in dry flour before boiling.

TO KEEP CAULIFLOWER WHITE
Boil upside-down, with stalk uppermost, to prevent the scum from discoloring the "flower." Alternatively, wrap in muslin before cooking; or cook in half milk and half water, uncovered, until just tender.

TO KEEP PARSLEY GREEN
After chopping, wrap the parsley in a piece of linen or the corner of a towel, then wash in cold water and squeeze dry. Alternatively, dip parsley in boiling water before chopping.

NEW VEGETABLES FOR OLD

If vegetables have become wilted or withered, all is not lost: the secret skills of the cook may help to bring new life to them, and make them palatable once more.

TO FRESHEN ASPARAGUS
To freshen tired asparagus, place with the stems in cold water for a while.

TO FRESHEN ROOT AND LEAF VEGETABLES
Ageing root vegetables become wrinkled, and leaf vegetables wilt. To revive tired vegetables, stand them in very cold salted water.

TO BRING BACK FLAVOR
To restore the sweetness of youth to old vegetables, add a little sugar to the water while cooking.

TO COOK OLD CARROTS
Grate them, and place in a basin with a teaspoon of butter and half a cup of milk. Cover the basin and steam the carrots until tender.

VEGETABLE VARIETY

When winter strikes and fresh vegetables are scarce, or if you have simply become bored with the usual roots and greens, try these suggestions:

BUTTERED SPINACH RIBS
The ribs of spinach leaves should be removed, as they become stringy when cooked. The ribs of spinach beet and seakale beet, however, can be used to make a delectable dish. Chop them into pieces, cook, and serve tossed in butter.

BUTTERED BRUSSELS TOPS
In the winter, Brussels sprouts may appear on the table with monotonous regularity. To vary the diners' diet, other parts of the plant may be used. The tops may be cooked with half their weight in onions, and served with a generous coating of butter. This dish has all the taste and texture of a dish of creamy leeks.

SALADS

TO SEPARATE LETTUCE LEAVES
Cut out the core of the lettuce and place it under running water, so the water runs into the cavity. Drain and dry the leaves before using.

TO DRY LETTUCE OR OTHER SALAD GREENS
Wash and place damp leaves in a dishcloth. Hold the edges of the cloth together to enclose the lettuce, and shake vigorously. Excess dampness will be absorbed by the dishcloth.

TO CRISP CELERY
Take apart and clean, then place in a jug of cold water containing a teaspoonful of salt or powdered borax, and leave for several hours. Alternatively, let the celery stand in cold water to which 1 teaspoon of sugar per quart has been added.

FRUIT

TO RETAIN JUICE IN BERRIES
Wash strawberries and raspberries, and other berries, *before* you hull them, so you won't wash out the juice.

TO PEEL ORANGES AND GRAPEFRUIT
To make the peel easier to remove, leave the fruit to stand in boiling water for about eight minutes.

TO REMOVE CHERRY PITS
Insert a new nib into an old-fashioned penholder, with the pointed end in, and take out pits with the rounded end. Or use the curved end of a clean unused hairpin.

TO PREVENT CUT FRUITS FROM DISCOLORING
As soon as you have cut the fruit, sprinkle the cut surfaces with lemon or pineapple juice.

TO AVOID WRINKLED SKINS ON BAKED APPLES
If you want your baked apples to come out of the oven smooth and unbroken, slit the skins in a few places before baking.

USING ROTTEN APPLES

Rotten apples aren't edible – but can be put to good use, as one seventeenth-century cider-maker found:

"A convenient quantity of rotten apples mixed with the sound is greatly assistant to the work of fermentation, and notably helps to clarify the cider. A friend of mine having made provision of apples for cider, whereof so great a part were found rotten when the time for grinding them came that they did (as it were) wash the room with their juice, had cider from them not only passable but exceeding good."

From OBSERVATIONS ON CIDER by JOHN NEWBURGH, 1678

EXTRACTING JUICE

TO EXTRACT JUICE FROM LEMONS

To get as much juice as possible from lemons, heat the fruit before squeezing.

TO EXTRACT A SMALL AMOUNT OF LEMON JUICE

If you want just a small amount of juice from a lemon, puncture the skin with a fork and gently squeeze out the amount required.

EXTRACTING ONION JUICE

Cut a slice from the root end and scrape the juice from the center with the edge of a teaspoon.

MILK

TO MAKE SWEET MILK SOUR

Add 2 tablespoons of lemon juice or vinegar to each cup of sweet milk.

TO WHIP EVAPORATED MILK

Place the can in the freezing unit of your refrigerator, and leave it there until the milk is partly frozen. Pour it into a very cold bowl, add 1 tablespoon of lemon juice to every ⅔ cup of milk, then whip like cream.

BUTTER & SHORTENING

TO CUT CLEANLY
Cover the blade of the knife with waxed paper, or heat it in hot water before cutting the butter.

TO MEASURE LESS THAN A CUP
When a recipe calls for less than a cup of butter or shortening, you can measure the right quantity by simply working out the difference between 1 cup and the amount of fat needed. For example, if ¼ cup is required, the difference would be ¾ cup. Pour the equivalent amount of water into a cup (in this case, three-quarters). Add butter or shortening until the water reaches the top of the cup – then pour off the water before using the fat.

TO DECORATE BUTTER
Cut butter into squares. Dip a fork into hot water and run the tines across the butter. Garnish with a sprig of fresh parsley.

TO MAKE BUTTER BALLS
Scald a pair of wooden butter paddles and place them in iced water for about an hour. Take tablespoonfuls of firm (but not hard) butter, and roll lightly between the paddles with a circular motion to form balls. Drop them on to a chilled plate, or a bed of cracked ice, or into iced water. To make rolls of butter, flatten the butter into cylinders, instead of shaping it into balls.

TO MAKE BUTTER CURLS
Have the butter firm but not hard. Dip your butter curler into hot water. Beginning at the far end of the slab of butter, draw the curler lightly and quickly towards you to make a thin shaving that curls up. Repeat, dipping the curler into hot water each time, until you have sufficient curls, then chill.

TO MOLD BUTTER
Scald fancy butter molds, then place in iced water for one hour. Fill with butter, levelling off the top. Press out butter and chill.

FAT

REMOVING FROM SOUP OR STOCK
For a low-fat soup or stock, strain the soup or stock while still hot through a cold, wet cloth.

USING UP WASTE FAT
Cut any pieces – raw or cooked – into cubes, place them in an iron pan and cover with cold water. Allow the water to boil, skimming occasionally, until the liquid is reduced to less than one third of its original volume. Strain it into a bowl, and leave to become cold. The fat will then set in a layer at the top, and can be easily taken off and used for frying, or other forms of cooking.

CLARIFYING
Melt the fat in a pan, then add slices of potato and fry until the potato is brown. The potato will absorb any foreign flavors and will collect some of the sediment.

CREAM

TO WHIP CREAM
To make cream whip more easily, add a few drops of lemon juice, and chill thoroughly before whipping.

TO THICKEN
If cream is not thick enough to beat for decorative purposes, whip the white of one or more eggs with it, according to the quantity required.

TO MAKE SWEET CREAM SOUR
Add 2 teaspoons lemon juice or 1 teaspoon vinegar to each cup of cream.

CREAM SUBSTITUTE
Beat together ½ oz caster sugar and the whites of two eggs, till light and frothy. This makes a good topping for fruit, or for sweet pies.

EGGS

FROM THE REFRIGERATOR
Remove eggs from the refrigerator long enough before using to allow them to reach room temperature. If you need to separate eggs, this is easiest to do as soon as the eggs have come out of the fridge.

TO BEAT THE WHITE
When half beaten, add a pinch of cream of tartar. This prevents the white falling.

TO MAKE MERINGUE
For really airy meringue, make sure that the bowl and whisk are scrupulously clean and there is no yolk in the white – otherwise the white will produce less bulk.

TO PREVENT MERINGUE FROM SHRINKING
To prevent a pie topping from shrinking, spread the meringue out so it covers the edge of the pie shell. Bake for 15 to 20 minutes in a slow oven (325°F).

TO BEAT EGGS FOR CAKES AND PUDDINGS
When beating whole eggs for cakes or puddings, add a pinch of bicarbonate of soda instead of salt. This makes the eggs froth up more quickly and gives them, and your cake or pudding, a richer color.

TO PREVENT CRACKING
To stop eggs cracking during boiling, dip them in cold water before placing them in the pan.

TO BOIL A CRACKED EGG
If an egg is already cracked and you want to boil it, smear the crack with butter, sprinkle on some salt, and wrap in greased paper. It will then be safe to boil.

TO HARD-BOIL EGGS FOR SALAD
Cook the eggs in boiling water for 12 minutes, then take them out and place them directly into cold water; this will stop an unattractive black ring forming around the yolks. To cut the eggs without breaking the yolks, dip the knife into hot water first.

TO WHITEN POACHED EGGS
When poaching eggs, drop a little vinegar into the water to preserve their whiteness. Adding vinegar also helps to stop them disintegrating during cooking.

TO DIVIDE A SINGLE EGG
When less than 1 egg is needed, beat it slightly so yolk and white mix, and measure out with a tablespoon.

SAVING EGGS

IN CAKES

If a cake requires more than three eggs, each additional egg can be replaced by 1 additional teaspoonful of baking powder and 1 teaspoonful of cornflour.

IN PUDDINGS

When making a pudding, you can use a dessertspoonful of cornflour in place of one of the eggs.

IN PUDDINGS AND CAKES

Instead of four eggs, dissolve 1 tablespoonful of golden syrup in ½ pint of warm milk, and add to the mixture before baking: this is excellent for binding. Remember that the syrup will add sweetening, so reduce the amount of sugar used.

IN CUSTARDS AND SAUCES

If more than two eggs are needed, omit all additional eggs and use instead 1 tablespoonful of cornflour for each egg omitted. The cornflour should first be blended with cold milk and brought to the boil before the eggs are added.

IN OMELETS AND SCRAMBLED EGGS

Increase bulk by adding 1 tablespoonful of milk or water for each egg used.

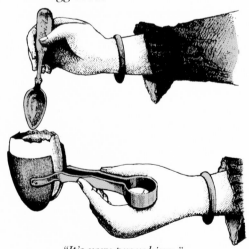

"It's very provoking,"
Humpty Dumpty said after a long silence,
"to be called an egg – very!"
From ALICE THROUGH THE LOOKING-GLASS by LEWIS CARROLL (1832-98)

SAUCES

Sauces are generally thickened with flour or eggs. Egg-based sauces, such as hollandaise and mayonnaise, can be quite tricky to make as the eggs may curdle.

TO SAVE A HOLLANDAISE SAUCE
Remove the sauce from the heat and add 1 teaspoon of cold water to every ½ pint of sauce.

An alternative remedy is to put another egg yolk into a clean bowl, add the separated sauce a little at a time, and place it over the hot water again to thicken gently. If the yolks have become so hot that they have turned into scrambled egg, the sauce cannot be saved.

TO SAVE MAYONNAISE SAUCE
The oil for making mayonnaise must be neither too hot nor too cold or it will curdle the sauce. If the oil has thickened in cold weather, bring it into a warm room to thaw gradually and do not use it until it is clear and liquid again; if it is too warm, cool it on ice before making the sauce. To save curdled mayonnaise, whisk a fresh yolk into a clean bowl and gradually whisk in the mayonnaise.

TO KEEP MAYONNAISE
To make mayonnaise keep for up to three days, at the very last moment add 2 tablespoonfuls of hot water to every ½ pint of sauce. Do not store homemade mayonnaise in the fridge.

TO THICKEN COOKED SAUCES
To make a smooth thickening agent, place some flour and water in a small jar, close with a lid, and shake well to mix. You can stir this into cooked sauces that have not thickened sufficiently. They then need to be cooked a little longer so the thickener can take effect.

CUSTARDS

TO PREVENT BURNING
Too much direct heat makes a custard curdle, so you need to place a dish or pan of water under the custard to help protect it. A pouring custard is best made in a *bain-marie* or double boiler – two saucepans fitted together with hot water in the bottom and the sauce in the top. When baking a custard in the oven, stand it in a dish of water.

TO TELL WHEN A CUSTARD IS THICK ENOUGH
Like other cooked sauces, a real egg custard is thickened by being heated. If your custard does not seem thick enough, you may be tempted to increase the heat – but you then risk curdling it. Here is a way of telling when your custard is ready.

Stir the custard quickly round and round in one direction, then remove the spoon; if the custard "turns back," instead of going the way it has been stirred, it is ready. It should quickly be poured into a cool bowl and stirred frequently while it is cooling.

TO SAVE A CUSTARD
Turn the curdled custard into a clean, cold bowl, and keep on stirring it one way until it is cold.

When Jacky's a good boy,
He shall have cakes and custard;
But when he does nothing but cry,
He shall have nothing but mustard.
NURSERY RHYME

JUNKET DAYS

In Britain, from the Middle Ages right through to the eighteenth century, junket (a delicately flavored milk pudding set with rennet) was an essential dish on every holiday and at every feast and fair. As a result, these special days came to be called "junket days" and people talked of going "a-junketing."

To make junket, milk was warmed to blood heat, and sugar, rennet, and any flavorings, such as rose water or spices, were stirred in. The pudding was then left in a cool place until the action of the rennet had set the milk. As a finishing touch, the junket might be covered with thick cream and sprinkled with nutmeg.

RENNET A setting agent derived from a calf's stomach lining.

TO MAKE FINE & CRISP PANCAKES

"To make fine pancakes fried without butter or lard. Take a pint of cream and six new-laid eggs, beat them very well together, put in a quarter of a pound of sugar and one nutmeg grated or a little mace (which you please) and so much flour as will thicken as much as ordinary Pancake batter. Your pan must be heated reasonable hot and wiped with a clean cloth: this done, put in the batter as thick or thin as you please."

From THE COMPLEAT COOK, 1671

"To make Pancakes so crisp that you may set them upright. Make a dozen or a score of them in a little frying pan, not bigger than a saucer: and then boil them in lard, and they will look as yellow as gold, besides the taste."

From THE NEWE BOOK OF COOKERIE, 1615

BREAD

TO CUT FRESH BREAD
Very fresh bread is soft and difficult to cut. Using a hot knife makes the job easier.

TO BUTTER BREAD FOR THIN SANDWICHES
Cut off the crust from one end of a loaf, then spread butter on the end of the loaf and cut a thin slice. Go on buttering and slicing as often as required. Slices of bread buttered and cut in this way are much less likely to tear or break.

TO FRESHEN ROLLS
To revive stale rolls, place them in a paper bag. Twist the top of the bag to close, and heat in a hot oven (400°F) for 15 minutes.

TO PREVENT TOAST FROM BECOMING SOGGY
When using toast as a base for a poached egg, remove the egg from the water with a pierced spoon or pancake turner and allow it to drain thoroughly before placing it on the toast.

TO MAKE BREAD CRUMBS
Force dry bread through a food processor, or place it in a small cloth bag and crush with a rolling pin.

TO MAKE A LARGE CROUSTADE
A croustade is a large bread case, which can be filled with a creamy filling. To make a croustade, cut crusts from a loaf of bread and remove the center, leaving walls and base about ¾ inch thick. Brush with butter inside and out, and toast. Smaller croustades can be made from sections of loaf.

TO MAKE BREAD TIMBALES
Timbales are cup-shaped molds, or the dishes cooked in them. To prepare quick timbales from bread, cut the crusts off squares of fresh bread, press into muffin pans and toast. The corners will turn up, and the timbales can then be filled as you choose.

PIES & PASTRY

TO PREVENT FRUIT FILLINGS FROM BOILING OVER
- Place a straw through a hole in the center of the pastry lid.
- Place a tiny funnel or 4-inch stick of uncooked macaroni in the center of the pie.
- Place a strip of dampened cloth or pastry tape around the edge of the pie.

TO PREVENT PASTRY SHRINKING
Roll out the pastry and place it in the pie pan without stretching it. Set the pastry aside for 5 minutes before fluting the edge.

DAINTY DISHES

Just as we now use kitchen foil to wrap foods during cooking, so early cooks used pastry. Originally a flour-and-water paste, pastry was not meant to be eaten but was used merely to seal in the juices of meat or game. Eventually, milk and fat were added, and edible pastry was created. In the Middle Ages, enormous pies were made. These were filled with meat, game, fish, or fruit, and had rich pastry cases known as "coffers." By the 1600s, pastrycooks had reached the peak of inventiveness in devising amazing puff and flaky pastries.

Sing a song of sixpence,
A pocket full of rye,
Four and twenty blackbirds,
Baked in a pie;
When the pie was opened,
The birds began to sing;
Was not that a dainty dish
To set before the king?
TRADITIONAL RHYME

LUCKY PIES

Mince pies, the small, round, spicy fruit pies that are
so much a part of British Christmas fare, were once
square, to represent Christ's manger. One traditional
belief maintains that you should eat mince pies made
by as many different cooks as possible, and for every
pie cooked by a different hand you will have a lucky
month in the coming year.

*"The best receipt [recipe] for Minced Pie mixture. One
pound of tripe well shred or thirteen eggs hard-boiled
with half the whites taken out; two pounds of suet well
shred as small as possible; one pound raisins; two
pounds of prunes stoned and shred; one pound
currants and half an ounce of nuts; cinnamon, mace
and cloves a quarter ounce each; eight sour apples
shred; one gill each of verjuice, sack and brandy; and
half a pound of lemon peel with sugar."*

From THE FAIRFAX HOUSEHOLD BOOK (17th/18th century)

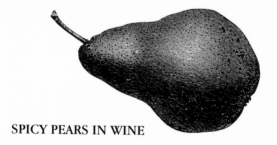

SPICY PEARS IN WINE

*"To stew wardens or pears. Peel them, put them into a
Pipkin, with so much Red or Claret-wine and water as
will near reach to the top of the Pears. Stew or boil
gently, till they grow tender, which may be in two
hours. After a while, put in some sticks of Cinnamon
bruised and a few Cloves. When they are almost done,
put in Sugar enough to season them well and their
Syrup, which you pour out upon them in a deep plate."*

From THE CLOSET OF SIR KENELM DIGBY OPENED, 1669

WARDENS Cooking pears.

PIPKIN Small pot-bellied
cooking pot.

TWELFTH NIGHT

Christmas and New Year celebrations traditionally end on the "Twelfth Day of Christmas" or "Twelfth Night" (January 6th). A special cake used to be baked to mark the occasion, with a pea and a bean hidden in it. Twelfth Night festivities were presided over by a couple known as the "King of the Bean" and "Queen of the Pea." If a man found the pea, then he chose the Queen. – but if a woman found the bean, it was her prerogative to choose the King; .

"To make a Twelfth Cake. Put two pounds of butter in a warm pan and work it to a cream with your hand: then put in two pounds of loaf sugar sifted; a large nutmeg grated; and of cinnamon ground, allspice ground, ginger, mace and coriander each a quarter ounce. Now break in eighteen eggs by one and one, meantime beating it for twenty minutes or above; stir in a gill of brandy: then add two pounds of sifted flour, and work it a little. Next put in currants four pounds, chopped almonds half a pound; citron the like; and orange and lemon peel cut small half a pound. Put in one bean and one pea in separate places, bake it in a slow oven for four hours, and ice it or decorate it as you will."

From THE EXPERIENCED ENGLISH HOUSEKEEPER
by ELIZABETH RAFFALD, 1769

SUGAR

TO SPRINKLE
If you haven't got a sugar dredger, you can use a salt shaker for sprinkling sugar – and also for mixtures of sugar with other ingredients (such as spices).

TO MOISTEN BROWN SUGAR
If brown sugar has become hard, place a slashed apple down one side of the jar in which the sugar is stored; place a slice of very moist bread on the other side, cover tightly and leave until the sugar is moist.

TO SAVE
When making fruit pies or puddings, or stewing fruit, put in $\frac{1}{4}$ teaspoonful of bicarbonate of soda for every 1 lb of fruit. This will save one third of the sugar you normally need. When stewing fruit, add the sugar only in the last 5 or 10 minutes.

RICE

TO SOFTEN RICE IN A PUDDING
Add a pinch of bicarbonate of soda to the dish along with the rice and sugar. This makes the rice soften more quickly, so it takes less time to cook.

TO KEEP WHITE
Add a few drops of lemon juice to the water in which rice is to be boiled. This will also separate the grains and make the rice more fluffy.

FLOUR

Flour should be perfectly dry when used for baking. If at all damp, the preparation is sure to be heavy.

TO ICE A CAKE

A little flour sprinkled over the top of a cake prevents the icing running down the sides.

TO FRESHEN SHREDDED COCONUT

Soak in milk until moist, adding some sugar if desired. Alternatively, place the coconut in a sieve, set it over boiling water, and steam until soft and moist.

TO ADD EXTRA FLAVOR TO DOUGHNUTS

Place a few whole cloves or a stick of cinnamon in the fat while frying.

CUTTING & DICING

Use kitchen shears to cut up parsley; to dice cooked meats or giblets; to cut crusts from bread; and to cut marshmallow, rhubarb, celery, etc.

THINKING AHEAD

FRENCH DRESSING
Heat 1 cup of vinegar and 1 peeled, crushed clove of garlic to boiling. Strain, add salt, pepper, and dry mustard, and store in a corked bottle. Add some of the mixture to oil whenever a dressing is needed.

WHITE SAUCE
Prepare a quantity of white sauce, pour it into a quart jar, cover, and store in the refrigerator. You will then have a supply of sauce to use as and when needed.

BISCUITS
If you want to serve hot biscuits for dinner, prepare them in the morning. Cut them into shapes, arrange on a baking sheet, and place in the refrigerator. About 20 minutes before you want to serve them, take the biscuits out of the fridge and bake them.

FINISHING TOUCHES

TO GARNISH LETTUCE LEAVES
Place paprika on waxed paper and dip the edges of the lettuce leaves into it.

TO FRILL CUCUMBERS
Draw a fork lengthwise down the middle of a cucumber. When you cut it crosswise into slices, they will have a "frilly" edge. Peeled bananas may be fluted in the same way.

TO MAKE CELERY CURLS
Cut the stalks lengthwise into thin strips, to within 1 inch of the end, and put them in iced water. Longer stalks may be curled at both ends.

TO MAKE PICKLE FANS
To make fan shapes from sweet pickles, cut each pickle into thin parallel slices, almost to the end. Spread and press the uncut end of the pickle carefully to hold the fan in place.

TO MAKE DECORATIVE CRACKER TOPPINGS
Press cheese or spreads through a pastry tube, or a funnel of heavy white paper, to create designs on top of the crackers.

CHAPTER FIVE

TO YOUR TASTE

THE SCENT OF GARLIC AND HERBS
and the aroma of spices can transform
a dull dish into something special. To please
the nose and the palate, the cook needs to know
which flavors make the happiest partners,
and how to bring out the taste of a dish by adding
"just a little something."

"Variety is the spice of life,
That gives it all its flavour."
From "THE TASK" by WILLIAM COWPER, 1731-1800

THE FIRST SEASONINGS

Early man may, by modern standards, have lived on a very crude diet, but even in those distant days, our ancestors were aware that seasoning their food made it taste better. Archeologists have found evidence that the seeds of certain plants were used in this way – mustard seed was chewed with meat, for example, and the toasted seeds of wild wheat and barley were sprinkled on other foods to add a nutty taste.

"I like, very much indeed, a little mustard with a bit of beef spread thinly under it; and I like brown sugar – only it should have some apple pudding mixed with it to keep it from being too sweet; but perhaps what I like best of all is salt, with some soup poured over it. The use of the soup is to keep the salt from being too dry; and it helps to melt it."

REVEREND CHARLES LUTWIDGE DODGSON, alias LEWIS CARROLL, 1878

"Being kissed by a man who didn't wax his moustache was . . . like eating an egg without salt."

From PLAIN TALES FROM THE HILLS by RUDYARD KIPLING (1865-1936)

SALT OF THE EARTH

Salt is important not only as a seasoning, but is also, in the correct quantity, essential for our health. So highly do we prize it that it has been used as an economical tool (the wealth of Venice was derived from trading in salt) and even as a political weapon (Mahatma Ghandi and his followers made sea salt "illegally" as a protest against British rule). Food without salt is considered by many to be not worth eating.

The value placed on salt is clearly shown in the old practice of seating people at table either "above" or "below" the salt. The salt was kept in a massive silver container known as a "saler," and this was placed in the center of the table. Guests of distinction were seated above the salt – between the salt cellar and the head of the table – and those who were considered less important, or inferior, were seated below the salt.

"Ye are the salt of the earth: but if the salt have lost his savour, wherewith shall it be salted?"
GOSPEL ACCORDING TO ST MATTHEW

PEPPER

"Of the various peppers that she [the housewife] will find useful, Paprika has recently achieved popularity in our kitchens. This is a red pepper – a very great deal less pungent than cayenne, and most attractive for flavouring. The Hungarian paprika is the best, the Spanish sort lacking flavour; it can be bought from most grocers. Cayenne pepper is of course too well-known to need description; but Nepaul Pepper is not so well-known: it has the pungency of cayenne but is yellowish in colour and more delicate in flavour. It need not perhaps be added that every kitchen should possess a wooden pepper-mill; for the freshly-ground pepper (more particularly when it is black) is vastly better than the kinds that are bought already ground. Unless you wish to use white pepper for the appearance of the dish, black pepper is always the finer-flavoured."
From THE CALENDAR OF COOKING, 1936

SAUCY SEASONING

Salt and pepper need not be the only staple seasonings. In Rome, for example, one of the most popular
seasonings was a sauce called *liquamen*. It was so
popular that it was even made in factories. This clear,
golden liquid was used in many different dishes, and
added a strongly salty, slightly fishy, and slightly
cheesy taste. It was made from fish, such as sprats,
anchovies, and mackerel, salted and left to ferment for
several months.

The nearest modern equivalent would be the oriental
fermented sauces known as *nam pla* in Thailand,
nuoc mam in Vietnam, and *tuk trey* in Cambodia. The
salt used in making *liquamen* played an important part
in keeping the balance between fishiness and cheesi-
ness. Modern Eskimos sometimes keep the fins, heads,
tails, and guts of fish in underground pits, where they
decompose into a mixture with a strong cheesy taste;
because no salt has been added, however, there is no
fishy flavor.

DO YOU TAKE SUGAR?

Sugar cane was probably originally a native of the Far
East, and has been cultivated in China for 2,000 years,
from where it gradually spread westwards. It was not
widely used in European cooking until the sixteenth
century. Before this time, the universal sweetener was
honey, or, to a lesser extent, fig syrup, date syrup, or
grape juice. On encountering sugar cane in India, an
admiral on the staff of Alexander the Great did not
know what these strange plants were, and said that he
had seen reeds that produced "honey" without bees.

With the spread of Islamic rule, sugar was cultivated
in North Africa, Sicily, and Spain. In 1471, a Venetian
discovered how to produce loaf sugar from raw,
brown sugar, and by the next century it had become
common in Europe.

SPICES OF THE EAST

While away on their campaigns in the Near East, the Crusaders were introduced to a whole new culinary experience. They carried many of their newly acquired tastes home, the most far-reaching of which was a liking for spices. Spices became invaluable in adding flavor and interest to the rather dreary basic diet of medieval Europe, which consisted of bread, beans, salted meat and dried fish.

Spices had two other big advantages – they could disguise any rancidity in fresh foods, and mask excess saltiness in salted meat and fish. Salt and spices were inseparable in the medieval diet: meat or fish preserved by salting needed bland accompaniments to offset the saltiness – and these in turn needed additional seasoning in the form of spices to give them flavor. From a modern cook's point of view, the food must have been greatly overseasoned.

EASY DOES IT

While seasonings can do much to enhance the flavor and appeal of a dish, it is important not to overdo it. Certain spices (such as nutmeg, for example) used too liberally can overpower and spoil a dish.

Nose, nose, jolly red nose,
And what gave you that jolly red nose?
Nutmeg and ginger, cinnamon and cloves,
That's what gave me this jolly red nose.
SEVENTEENTH-CENTURY SONG

THE SAUCEMAKER

Spicy sauces became very popular in medieval times, and diners would mop them up with mouthfuls of meat. In fact, they were so much in demand that in fourteenth-century Paris, housewives could buy sauces ready-made from professional saucemakers. There was "yellow sauce", flavored with ginger and saffron; "green sauce", flavored with ginger, cloves, cardamom, and green herbs; and, most popular of all, "cameline sauce", a kind of bread sauce flavored with cinnamon. One recipe for cameline was as follows:

"Take raisins of Corinth, and kernals of nuts, and crust of bread and powder of ginger, cloves, flour of cinnamon, pound it well together and add it thereto. Salt it, temper it up with vinegar, and serve it forth."
From THE FORME OF CURY, 1780

SPICED SALT

"The French use spices more freely than we do, especially in the preparation of meat dishes; and they have rather cunningly invented what they call SEL ÉPICÉ, *or as we should say 'spiced salt', which they mix in quantity and keep ready at hand ... This salt is always made in the same proportions ... ten parts of salt, two parts of pepper and one part of mixed spice."*
From THE CALENDAR OF COOKING, 1936

OVERCOMING SALTINESS

In medieval times, meat and fish were often salted to preserve them. When it came to cooking these foods, however, the cook had a problem – there was no ready supply of running water, and so there was no easy way to wash the salt out. The cook therefore had to invent other solutions. One trick was to suspend a cloth filled with oatmeal in the cauldron in which the meat was cooking, so the oatmeal absorbed the salt.

Another remedy was to serve the meat with a bland accompaniment that would offset the saltiness, such as a creamy sauce or starchy pudding. Such accompaniments included blamanger (a dish of chopped chicken or fish, thickened with ground almonds) and frumenty (a thick pudding made of grains and almond milk).

The Roman way with salt meat was to cook it first in milk, to make it sweet, and then in water.

BLAMANGER The name has evolved into the modern "blancmange" – a sweet, smooth molded dessert thickened with cornflour.

HOW TO MAKE A FRUMENTY

"To make a rich frumenty for ten persons. Steep one pound of whole grains of wheat in water overnight, and then boil the steeped grains in one pint of milk until the whole be soft. Add thereto raisins and sultanas, honey, a nutmeg freshly grated, a little cinnamon, brandy and cream: and serve it forth hot or cold."
From MISTRESS BARTON'S COOKERY BOOK, c.1680

SAVING SALTY SOUP

If you have added too much salt to a soup, add a piece of raw potato to it and boil for a few minutes. The potato will absorb some of the salt.

THE HERB GARDEN

Herbs have been grown by mankind for hundreds of years, for culinary use and – more importantly in the days before the invention of modern drugs – their medicinal and healing properties. In old gardens, there would be a section set aside for the growing of herbs. This delightful tradition is well worth continuing: what could be more satisfying than being able to pick fresh herbs from your own garden to add to the evening's meal? The aroma alone as you brush past the plants is a treat in itself.

The range of herbs is huge, and few of us nowadays will have either the space or the inclination to grow all the varieties found in the traditional herb garden. Nevertheless, a small bed of the more common herbs – or just a selection in pots on the windowsill – will help to give your cooking that old-fashioned, country flavor. Some herbs, such as rosemary, are perennial, and will go on growing for years; others, like parsley, are annual, so you will need to raise or buy fresh plants each year.

BASIL
Excellent with tomato salad, or in green salad.

CARAWAY
Use seeds in cakes, and in cheese and cabbage dishes.

CHERVIL
Use in salads and as a garnish.

CHIVES
The onion-flavored shoots are good in salads, and also in cooked egg dishes.

CORIANDER
Use coriander leaves to flavor soups and stews, and the seeds in curries.

DILL
Both the seeds and the leaves can be used; the mild aniseed flavor of dill is good with fish, or with bland savory dishes.

FENNEL
The aniseed flavor of the seeds is excellent with fish, particularly oily fish such as mackerel.

MARJORAM (OREGANO)
Has a great many different uses, but is especially good with tomatoes.

MINT
Excellent with fresh, young vegetables, such as new potatoes or peas.

PARSLEY
An essential herb with many different uses; chopped fine, it gives a fresh taste to salads.

ROSEMARY
A strongly aromatic herb, excellent with roast lamb.

SAGE
Use with fresh pork or pork sausages, or with earthy-flavored vegetables such as broad beans.

TARRAGON
Its sweet taste is superb with roast chicken.

THYME
The aromatic taste complements many foods, and gives an authentic flavor to Mediterranean dishes.

BOUQUET GARNI

"This consists invariably of two or three stalks of parsley, a sprig of fresh thyme and a half or a whole bayleaf. If the bouquet is to consist of other herbs, their names should be given. If the words bouquet garni are used simply, the above mixture is implied. If fresh thyme cannot be obtained, the dried sort may be used, in which case the bouquet will be tied up in a little bag of muslin, so that it can easily be withdrawn when necessary. If the herbs are fresh, the bouquet is tied round with cotton. The presence of these herbs in stock, or in various stews, etc., will make all the difference to the flavour."

From THE CALENDAR OF COOKING, 1936

FINES HERBES

This is the French name for a mixture of finely chopped, fresh herbs – parsley, chervil, chives, and tarragon. They can be used in delicate-tasting cooked dishes, or sprinkled over salads.

GARLIC

"Garlic . . . is a much maligned bulb, probably because when we taste garlic we do taste it indeed, and hardly anything else. But when it is properly used, and in very small quantities for our palates, it will give an indefinable taste which adds greatly to savour and richness . . . Many people like a cut clove of garlic lightly rubbed round the salad bowl before the salad is dressed, in the same way that others like to use an onion. It gives so much more delicate a flavour than the inclusion of the onion itself."

From THE CALENDAR OF COOKING, 1936

THE FIVE FLAVORS

Cooking is all about balance – balancing richness with tartness, sweet with savory, and complementary or contrasting textures. The characteristics of each dish were carefully distinguished by the ancient Chinese. With typical refinement, they divided them into five groups known as the "Five Flavors": thus a dish could be classified as bitter, salty, sour, hot, or sweet.

At one point, this idea even became the subject of philosophical debate: Taoist thinkers argued that the Five Flavors would eventually ruin the sense of taste, because using any sense to the full would dull it.

WHAT GOES WITH WHAT

Certain flavors have an affinity with certain foods:

- A little nutmeg perfectly complements the flavor of cheese sauce, white sauce, mashed potato, and spinach dishes.
- Grated orange and lemon rind, and cinnamon, make a delicious apple pie.
- Ginger is good with rhubarb, on fresh melon, or in cheesecake.
- A little sherry, added before serving, enhances the flavor of mushroom soup.
- Chocolate and chestnut make perfect partners, as do chocolate and orange.
- Salt brings out the flavor of certain fresh fruits, such as mangoes, pineapples, peaches, and nectarines.
- A little salt also enhances the flavor of homemade vanilla ice cream.

CHOCOHOLICS

"The Confection made of Cacao called Chocolate or Chocoletto, which may be had . . . in London at reasonable rates, is of wonderful efficacy for the procreation of children: for it not only vehemently incites to Venus, but causeth Conception in women . . . and besides that it preserves health, for it makes such as take it often to become fat and corpulent, fair and amiable."

From ADAM IN EDEN by WILLIAM COLES, 1657

BRINGING OUT THE FLAVOR

- Add a little strong coffee to a chocolate cake or pudding mix to intensify the chocolate flavor.
- Add a little sugar or grated orange rind to tomato sauces or soups.
- Add mustard to bring out the cheesy taste in a cheese sauce.

"If you beat spice, it will smell the sweeter."
TRADITIONAL SAYING

FLORAL FOOD

The delightful idea of using flowers as food is centuries old. In medieval times, cooks produced delicate rose-flavored sauces; Roman vintners steeped rose and violet petals in wine to impart a flowery bouquet; and fritters and flans of zucchini flowers are still an Italian delicacy. If you don't grow zucchini, then you can treat lilac, mimosa, or elder flowers in the same way. Nasturtiums are particularly useful: both the flowers and leaves can be eaten in salads, and the seeds can be pickled, rather like capers.

VIOLET SALAD

"Take a Batavian endive, some finely curled celery, a sprinkling of minced parsley, a single olive, and the petals of a couple of dozen blue violets. These several ingredients are to be mixed with the purest olive oil, salt and pepper being the only condiment. Add a dash of Bordeaux wine and a suspicion of white vinegar."
From MEALS MEDICINAL by DR W. T. FERNIE, 1905

SALAD WITH NASTURTIUMS

"Put a plate of flowers of the nasturtium in a salad bowl, with a tablespoonful of chopped chervil; sprinkle over with your fingers half a teaspoonful of salt, two or three tablespoonfuls of olive oil, and the juice of a lemon; turn the salad in the bowl with a spoon and fork until well mixed, and serve."

From the TURKISH COOKERY BOOK by TURABI EFENDI, 1864

PLANNING A TASTEFUL DINNER PARTY

The famous French gourmet and writer Jean Anthelme Brillat-Savarin had his own rules for planning a dinner party. No fewer than 12 people should be invited, and they should have different occupations but similar interests and tastes, so that the business of getting conversations going will be easier. The men should be witty, and the women not too prone to flirting.

As for the dining room, it should be well lit and maintained at a temperature of 65-68°F throughout the proceedings. There should be few dishes, and these should be served in a leisurely way, accompanied by fine wines. Coffee and liqueurs should follow the meal, and the guests should be led to a drawing room large enough for the dual activities of conversation and playing cards. Things should be so arranged that guests do not begin to leave before 11 o'clock, but by midnight everyone is tucked up in bed.

BIBLIOGRAPHY & ACKNOWLEDGMENTS

**The author and publishers
gratefully acknowledge the following:**

Art for Commerce, Scolar Press 1973
Book of Household Management, Isabella Beeton, S. O. Beeton 1861
(reprinted by Chancellor Press 1982)
Brewer's Dictionary of Phrase and Fable, compiled by
Rev. Ebenezer Cobham Brewer, Cassell 1968
Culinary Craft, ed. Ruth Berolzheimer, Consolidated Book Publishers 1942
The Dover Pictorial Archive Series
The Encyclopaedia of Illustrations, Studio Editions 1990
Encyclopedia of International Cooking, Colour Library Books 1988
The Everyman Dictionary of Quotations and Proverbs, compiled by
D. C. Browning, Chancellor Press 1982
Food in History, Reay Tannahill, Eyre Methuen 1973
(reprinted by Paladin Books 1975)
French Provincial Cooking, Elizabeth David, Michael Joseph 1986
Grandmother's Secrets, Jean Palaiseul, Penguin Books 1976
The International Thesaurus of Quotations, ed. Rhoda Thomas Tripp, Crowell 1970
(reprinted by Penguin Books 1976)
Mrs Beeton's Cookery Book, Isabella Beeton, Ward Lock 1914
Pleyn Delit, Constance B. Hiett & Sharon Butler, University of Toronto Press 1976
The Cookery Year, Reader's Digest Books 1975
The Country Housewife's Handbook,
West Kent Federation of Women's Institutes 1974
The National Mark Calendar of Cooking,
Ambrose Heath & D. D. Cottington Taylor, Ministry of Agriculture 1936
The "Olio" Cookery Book (revised edition), L. Sykes, Ernest Benn 1928
The Oxford Book of Nursery Rhymes, ed. Iona & Peter Opie,
Oxford University Press 1969
The Oxford Dictionary of Quotations, Oxford University Press 1948
The Perpetual Almanack of Folklore, Charles Kightly, Thames & Hudson 1987
The Roman Cookery Book, Barbara Flower & Elisabeth Rosenbaum, Harrap 1974
The Scots Kitchen, F. Marian McNeill, Blackie 1929 (reprinted 1955)
Sears Roebuck 1908 Catalogue (reprinted by DBI Books 1971)
The Vegetarian Epicure, Anna Thomas, Penguin Books 1984
Traditional British Cooking, Elisabeth Ayrton & Theodora Fitzgibbon,
Octopus Books 1985
The Victorian Catalogue of Household Goods, Studio Editions 1991

Jacket quotation: Harriet Van Horne, *Vogue*, 15 October 1956

"Kissing don't last: cookery do!"
From THE ORDEAL OF RICHARD FEVERAL by
GEORGE MEREDITH (1828-1909)